FINDING FABULOUS

Paving the Path Between Paycheck & Passion

by
Lisa Dadd

Finding Fabulous: Paving the Path between Paycheck and Passion by Lisa Dadd

Copyright © 2015 by Lisa Dadd

All rights reserved.

No part of this book may be reproduced in any written, electronic, recording, or photocopying without written permission of the publisher or author. The exception would be in the case of brief quotations embodied in the critical articles or reviews and pages where permission is specifically granted by the publisher or author.

If you would like to do any of the above, please seek permission first by contacting the author at www.lisadadd.com

Although every precaution has been taken to verify the accuracy of the information contained herein, the author and publisher assume no responsibility for any errors or omissions. No liability is assumed for damages that may result from the use of information contained within.

Published in Canada
ISBN 978-0-9948380-0-1 (paperback)
ISBN 978-0-9948380-1-8 (mobi)
ISBN 978-0-9948380-2-5 (epub)

Copyeditor: Beth Riley
Back Cover Photo: Art and Soul Photography
Cover Design: Suzana Stankovic
Interior Design: Zakira Karthigeyan
Ebook Formatting/Conversion: www.fromprinttoebook.com

Dedication

This book is dedicated to all the brave souls out there, defying the status quo, redefining what's possible and paving the way for the rest of us, as they persistently choose to live life on their own terms.

Contents

Foreword 9

Introduction 11

Section I: Pick your Path

Chapter 1: Road to Freedom 21
Yearning for Freedom 23
Freedom to Change 33
Roadmap: March toward Freedom 35

Chapter 2: Driven by Purpose 39
Defining Purpose 43
Pathways to Purpose 44
Roadmap: Design a Path of Purpose 58

Section II: Potholes & Pitfalls

Chapter 3: You 67
The Biggest Roadblock: You 68
Awareness—Do you know what you want? 70
Value—What do you have to offer? 76

Credibility—What will everyone think? 82

Confidence—Are you capable? 85

Faith—Do you believe it's possible? 88

Roadmap: Get Out of Your Own Way 92

Chapter 4: Money 97

What is money worth to you? 99

Key Influencers 101

Want vs. Need 111

Willingness 117

Roadmap: Show Me the Money 126

Chapter 5: Support 133

Weaving a Tapestry of Support 135

Types of Support 138

Levels of Support 145

Stages of Support 149

Mediums of Support 152

Naysayers & Negative Nellies 153

Roadmap: Build a Team of Allegiance 157

Chapter 6: Environment 163

The Ideal Environment 166

People – Whom do you want to work with? 167

Places – Where do you work? 173

Compensation – How do you like to be recognized? 181

Expression – Do you get to be you? 187

Roadmap: Design An Environment to Thrive In 193

Section III: Payoffs

Chapter 7: Signs of Success 199
Identify Influencing Factors 201
Redefine What It Means to Be Successful 212
Recognize & Celebrate... 217
Roadmap: Success in *Finding Fabulous* 224

Chapter 8: Highway to Happiness... 229
Meaning & Impact 231
Finding Happiness 238
Importance of Checkpoints... 243
Roadmap: Finding Happiness Along the Way........................ 247

Conclusion 251

Acknowledgements... 255

About the Author... 259

Finding FabFinders... 261

Foreword

Some people may call it brave, courageous, or even inspirational; others may think I was crazy or simply foolish. The decision to leave a successful, stable, high-paying job—with no idea what I was going to do next—could be considered any one of those things. How had I gotten here? When did my career (and more importantly, my life) get so off course? How many years had I been frustrated, unhappy, and unfulfilled in my job?

In my search for answers, I went looking for brave souls who risked everything to find more "fabulous." I didn't look for celebrities or hunt down the richest of the rich. I wanted to speak to the ordinary ones. I wanted to connect with the average, everyday, "just like you and me" kind of people who dared to defy the status quo. I wanted to understand how the average person could transform not only her job, but also her life.

In **Finding Fabulous**, I share stories of actual individuals who turned in their day jobs in order to find more meaning, purpose, and fun. Providing insights to the motivating factors that led them to risk it all and revealing the biggest challenges, I learned what they were able to accomplish and how their definition of success evolved along the way.

Essentially, **Finding Fabulous** is about individuals intentionally designing a more fabulous way of being and endeavouring to be it, in all aspects of their lives. May their real-life stories raise your awareness of possibilities and inspire you to consider the relevance to your own life.

Introduction

If I had to pinpoint the moment—the exact moment—when I knew my life was about to change course completely, I would pick that sunny afternoon in late August 2012. It was a split-second decision, years in the making. Standing on the cold hardwood floor in the middle of my kitchen, contemplating what to do with my life, the answer crashed into me: "Go! It's time to go!"

Despite feeling more than a little guilty for not being satisfied with my enviable job and all its associated perks, I couldn't shake the feeling that my career aspirations, and in essence my life aspirations, were less than admirable. I was playing small and I knew it! Standing in the kitchen that August morning, it became obvious that it was time to do something about it. And so—I decided to leave.

With that revelation, a new level of excitement and freedom arose inside of me. I felt like I was vibrating from a newfound energy source. Initially, I thought it was fear or uncertainty. But I wasn't uncertain. In fact, I was the most certain I had been in a long time. Odd, considering I had no idea what I was going to do! But it's true. I felt free and full of possibilities – and that somehow overshadowed my fears and doubts. Amazing! Had I known just how powerful that decision would be, maybe I wouldn't have waited so long to make it.

For several years, I had been making excuses for why I was living my career by default, telling myself, "When I figure out what I want to do, I'll go do it!" When the work got stagnant or the purpose misaligned with my values, I shrugged it off as a necessary compromise that comes with working in a large corporation. When I struggled to communicate with my boss or collaborate with my colleagues, I assumed it would get better. But most of the time, I ignored the ache in my gut and numbness in my soul. I just kept plugging along.

Then, just months before that fateful decision, I learned the company I worked for was about to undergo its third downsizing in five years. Suddenly everyone was more afraid of losing their jobs than doing their jobs, and attentions shifted to gossip and rumours about the downsizing. It was a contagiously toxic environment. Yet through all of it, I realized something surprising: I was more afraid of keeping my job than losing it! What did that say about me? How could I possibly stay after that truth bomb hit?

Just days after declaring my intention to leave, I sat at a boardroom table with several of my colleagues. As I listened to my boss explain the timeline for the impending downsizing, I discreetly scanned the solemn faces around the table. Everyone was so stressed and anxious! There was a palpable discomfort, a heaviness, in the room. That was perhaps the moment when the seeds for this book were planted. Why, when the environment was so toxic to so many of the people sitting around me, didn't more people take control of the decision? Why were they waiting for someone else to decide their fates and their futures? Why wouldn't (or couldn't) they look at their situations and realize they weren't happy any more (as many of them obviously weren't)?

A few months later, those questions echoed in my brain even more loudly, and my need for answers became more persistent, when I attended a business-networking event. As I listened intently to the stories that led each person to the group, I was surprised to hear how many of them had left corporate jobs to pursue their passions, escape the entrapment of corporate bureaucracy, or find more meaning in their lives. I heard about an engineer who decided to walk away from her career to become a horse therapist and a judge who traded her gavel for the opportunity to inspire athletes. There was a former radio producer who left mainstream media to spread more positive messages and an architect who decided he'd rather inspire people. So why did they do it? What motivated them to take the leap of faith? They all seemed to come from "successful," lucrative careers in areas like teaching, law, engineering, and business. Why did they dare to expect more from their work and their lives?

These stories provided a stark contrast to the conversations I'd had with people who were stuck in "job misery"—the folks who gave me a plethora of answers, excuses, barriers, and objections to the notion of going after their passions and fulfilling their dreams. The ones who claimed there was nothing else they could do, or that they wouldn't be able to pay their bills. They insisted responsibilities to spouses and children made the choice "unrealistic." Some thought they were too old or too inexperienced in anything other than their field. They blamed where they lived or the state of the economy for their perceived lack of options.

But what about those individuals I met who were finding ways to work toward better lives? Didn't they have similar issues and barriers to overcome? The police officer I met who worked and attended school (both full-time) to earn a degree and, eventually, his medical license—surely that couldn't have been easy! Didn't he have a family to support and self-confidence issues to overcome? There was an HR director with four kids and a stay-at-home wife: how did he manage to afford going after his dreams? What did his family's life look like while he figured it out? What about the lawyer who gave up her breadwinning salary and designer handbags in exchange for a good night's sleep? How did her definition and expectation of success change as she went through the process? What does success look like for all these people?

In my own search for clarity, I decided to focus on finding the answers to these questions. I wanted to know if this whole idea of "finding your passion" or "living your best life" is real. If it is, what does that even mean? I needed to quiet my fears of the unknown and get a "heads up" about what was coming. I wanted to learn from these people and their mistakes to better prepare for my own. I wanted their stories to inspire me and expand my perception of possible. But most of all, I wanted to know that I wasn't alone on this journey. So I went looking for brave souls who risked everything to find more "fabulous."

Now, I know that, just as many people never endeavour to run a four-minute mile, summit Mt. Everest or run for President of the United States, there are many who never endeavour to *find fabulous*. Sure, most people *wish* or *hope* for a fabulous life, but many won't invest the time and energy or take the steps required to actually realize it. With that in mind, I'd like to introduce you to a unique set of individuals I found. I call them FabFinders.

FabFinders are the brave souls I interviewed for this book, along with many others I spoke to over the past several years, who dared to leave their day jobs behind to pursue their passions, find more freedom, or connect with more meaning. Whether initially intentional or not, their desire to shift their careers became the catalyst for transforming their lives. In addition to changing where their paychecks came from, they rediscovered what they want from life and how they contribute to the world. Their decisions to have, do, and be *more* led them to test their own potential and discover a new perception of what's possible.

When I spoke to them, each was at a different stage of the journey. A few of them had just made the decision to go down the path, some were already on it, and still others were "on the other side," redefining a new phase of *Fabulous*. Some were like well-trained athletes who'd taken many steps throughout the years, and others were just finding their stride. Some took well-worn, seemingly familiar paths, while others cut their own through dense fields of newly discovered territory. Though our experiences will be as varied as each of theirs, the insights they offer pave the path and ease our way. The reasons they chose to go on the journey, the challenges they faced along the way, and the evolution of their definitions of success leave footprints that can help to guide us on our own paths to *Fabulous*.

Probing for answers to my questions, and looking deeper to appreciate the ones they weren't divulging, I began to see patterns emerge. I started to weave together the strings of seemingly unrelated tales. Perhaps that's where I found the most magic: insights hidden somewhere between their certainties and their optimisms—the really juicy stuff that might have been eluding even them. They acknowledged their greatest struggles and confessed their highest hopes, and in so doing revealed the wisdom of their journey and the heart of their souls. They provided evidence that courage of conviction is rewarded with *Finding Fabulous*, not in a particular place, but within one's self.

Equipped with the insights and wisdom procured from their stories, I find myself eager to share. For all of those wondering if there is a more fabulous life out there, I want to raise awareness of possibilities. For those ready to leave ordinary behind in search of your own version of *fabulous*, I want to offer the daring leaps of faith as evidence that it can be done. For anyone struggling to overcome barriers that threaten to stall your progress, I want to present creative solutions from those who have gone before. And for all those curious to know whether success is more than a statement in a bankbook, I want these stories to defy traditional definitions of what it means to be successful.

To help you get started on your path to *Finding Fabulous*, I've distilled the lessons I've learned into specific steps you can take right now. At the end of each chapter, you'll find a Roadmap—questions and exercises that will help you apply these ideas directly to your own life. If you are ready to dig in and start doing the work, download your free copy of the companion workbook at www.lisadadd.com/free-workbook/

Don't get me wrong—the point of this book isn't to tell you what *fabulous* is for you. It isn't to judge whether you or anyone else qualifies as living fabulously. I leave that up to you to decide for yourself. If I could have just one wish for you, it is that the messages, stories, and examples in this book will dare you to consider their relevance to your own life and challenge you to ask the questions:

>What does living a *fabulous life* mean to me?
>Am I living my version of a fabulous life?
>(And, if not…)
>What am I waiting for?

Although years have passed since that fateful morning in August, my journey of *Finding Fabulous* is far from over. The more steps I take toward the light of possibilities, the more certain I am that I'm on the right path. And though the path is winding and by no means easy, I know it is worth it. I know I'd rather brave the journey than settle for the alternative. I know that *Finding Fabulous* is a mindset more than an actual place or thing. And I think I've always known, deep in my heart, that choosing to take the first step meant I had already found it.

May the stories in this book help you take your first steps and encourage you to keep going down the path toward your fabulous life!

Section I: Pick your Path

Every morning in Africa, a gazelle wakes up.

It knows it must run faster than the fastest lion or it will be killed.

Every morning a lion wakes up.

It knows it must outrun the slowest gazelle or it will starve to death.

It doesn't matter whether you are a lion or a gazelle:

When the sun comes up, you'd better be running.

Dan Montano

As many times as I've heard that fable, it has only recently come to have new meaning for me. I used to think it was all about action: no matter what the situation is, or what happens, just keep moving. Now, though, I understand the advantage that both the lion and the gazelle have over most of us. Whether running away from pain (the gazelle) or toward pleasure (the lion), they are both very clear about *why* they run.

For a long time I wasn't running. I was grazing in the pasture of a corporate world. Numbed by financial incentives and distracted by the complacency of the herd around me, the pain of the situation didn't register.

It didn't occur to me to run, because I never slowed down long enough to consider what I was running toward. What did I want bad enough to cause me to act?

My first objective for interviewing the FabFinders was to understand their motivation to risk their seemingly good lives for something better. Why do they, when so many other people settle for less than fabulous, or even suffer in their circumstances? Why do they, when following the status quo could be so much "easier"?

As I listened to their stories, it became clear that their journeys were not instigated by any single variable. They weren't all suffering a mid-life crisis; they weren't even of similar ages. They weren't all struggling for money, nor did they all have excessive disposable incomes. They hadn't all gone to the same school of thought, or been raised by parents with the same child-rearing philosophies. They weren't all spiritually driven, nor did they share the same idea of what *Finding Fabulous* means. They did, however, all have one thing in common: each of them had a clear understanding of *why* they were risking it all.

As varied as their explanations were, two common themes seemed to come up time and time again. One of the most powerful words I heard in the interviews was *freedom*. In one form or another, FabFinders wanted more freedom. Whether they wanted more freedom with time, money, creative expression, or something else, it was a strong catalyst for change. Just as enticing was the drive to live with more *purpose*. Although each person described the concept of a purpose-driven life differently, the stimulus was no less influential.

Whether freedom or purpose dominated the FabFinders' decisions, the motivation to change was strong, and, more often than not, that sense of clarity seemed to act as the stimulus for their journey.

In this first section, we will explore the two most prominent motivators of change I encountered in my interviews with the FabFinders.

Motivations for Change:

- Freedom
- Purpose

The point of these two chapters is not to assume that you require more freedom or purpose in your life; I leave that decision up to you. However, I will propose that the power of clarity around your motivation for change is threefold: it acts as a catalyst for initiating that change, encourages you as you go through the change, and helps filter the decisions you will need to make as you move forward.

The personal stories of the FabFinders illustrate how one can leverage that clarity in order to design an ideal work environment and, ultimately, find a more fabulous life in general. The questions at the end of each section are designed to help you consider the relevance to your own journey.

How can you leverage your motivation for change on your journey of *Finding Fabulous*?

Chapter 1: Road to Freedom

Caged birds accept each other but flight is what they long for.

Tennessee Williams

Imagine for a moment that you were born and raised in a single room. It's a fine enough room, with all the essentials you need to survive, and it's been a decent enough environment to grow up in. You've never tried to get out of your room or even given much thought to how you could. Sure, there have been times when you felt limited by its walls and confined by the lack of windows and doors, but what could you do? It isn't as if you had another option. Then one day you wake up, and as your eyes start to regain focus, you catch a glimpse of a crack in one of the walls. Upon further inspection, you realize the crack is really a doorframe. You start to wonder how long that door has been there and why you never noticed it before.

Over the next few years, you start wondering what's on the other side of that door. You were satisfied enough when there wasn't another option, but this new realization descends upon you, and you suddenly feel trapped. You start thinking about all the things you would like to do or to have, if only you could get past that darn door! It becomes increasingly frustrating, the only thing you can think of. How did I get here? Why am I stuck here? What am I missing on the other side?

Eventually, you get to the point where you want to kick that door down. You think about the consequences for a moment, but you're so frustrated that you just can't stop yourself. Putting your scepticism aside, you march over, yank the handle, and—to your utter surprise—it opens!

In that moment you have to come to terms with two things. First, you've been "stuck" in that room all this time, believing you had little control over your situation, but that door was there the whole time, and it wasn't even locked. Second, despite the freedom you feel after finally being able to cross through that doorway, you suddenly realize you have no idea what you'll find on the other side. What if it isn't as nice and comfortable? What if you can't handle whatever is out there? What if, once you leave, you can never come back to the familiar, safe space you've always known?

And so you have a choice: you can stay in that small, limited, closed-in space you've known for years, or you can brave the unknown and walk toward "what could be."

It may seem absurd to think of someone being raised in a single room most of her life, never having the inclination to leave. But think about it: is it really any more absurd than someone who stays in a miserable job for years and years, insisting he or she "can't" leave? I mean, how many true cases of "can't" do you know? How many reasons couldn't be debated because of "too afraid," "unwilling," or "won't"? How different is the miserable employee from the one-room occupant in their perceptions of what it means to be "trapped"?

Reflecting back on my experiences in the corporate world, I see so many parallels. I remember the excitement of landing that first job and knowing the salary would free me from the prison of student loans. I believed that if I stayed put, I'd have all the essentials I needed to survive. I wasn't looking for an exit door. As the years passed by, and I started to see cracks in the walls of my desire to stay in that "safe" job, I'd hear colleagues say things like, "Who else is going to pay you what you get paid to do what you do?" They might as well have been saying, "Just stay here in this nice safe room—it's not as if you can leave anyway." Perhaps that's why I stopped looking around at what I might have been missing. I wasn't looking out the window for options or searching for the doorway that led to other possibilities (at least not outside the corporation where I worked).

So maybe it isn't too surprising that I had my own "want to kick the door down" moment. Once I saw the possibilities for more autonomy and creative expression, I began to realize that I didn't have to be limited by my circumstance, and I wanted out. Standing on the threshold between the safety of my company and what could be, I too felt the fear of the unknown.

Yearning for Freedom

> *The only way to deal with an unfree world is to become so absolutely free that your very existence is an act of rebellion.*
>
> **Albert Camus**

What does it mean to have more "freedom"? Whether they used the actual word "freedom" or implied the concept in the descriptions of their longings and desires, at some point almost everyone I interviewed expressed a need for more freedom. What freedom looked like varied for each person, and it was often expressed in divergent ways; it meant completely different things for the mother of young children, the young entrepreneur, and the veteran of corporate bureaucracy. However, whether the FabFinders sought more freedom with their time, finances, creative expression, or just freedom to decide on the quality and environment of their work lives, they shared a common sense of being trapped that ultimately became a key driver for change.

A thirty-nine-year-old HR director and father of four told me he felt so trapped by his job that he would go into his office and cry. An office administrator who later started her own personal fitness training business told me how she felt nauseated every day as she entered her office building. One teacher spoke about how confining it was to teach a mandated curriculum because it contradicted the understanding she gained through years of experience: that her students had different needs. Another teacher spoke about her limited ability to enjoy her own kids because of the time and energy she spent each day with other people's children.

So why was it so painful? Why did they feel so trapped?

As I delved deeper to try and understand their true motivation for change, I learned that the FabFinders essentially longed for freedom in one or more of three main areas:

- **Freedom of Time**
- **Financial Freedom**
- **Freedom of Expression**

The desire for freedom surfaced frequently in my interviews, but even more fascinating was the way the FabFinders leveraged that desire to propel themselves forward. In essence, it became the force they used to "kick down the door" and step into their new lives.

The intention of this chapter is to encourage you to consider various types of freedom and contemplate how more of it might impact your life. I won't propose that everyone longs for the same type of freedom, or even defines it in the same way; however, I do believe there is value in exploring what it could mean in our own lives.

How would your life look and feel if you had more freedom? Does the thought of it motivate you enough to start your own journey? What would it take for you to walk through your personal doorway toward the freedom of possibility?

Freedom of Time

Lost time is never found again.

Benjamin Franklin

Let's assume for a moment that you are brave enough to walk out of that room toward what "could be." In an effort to help you out, I'm going to give you a bank account filled with a set amount of money every day. The only caveat:

at the end of the day the money will be gone, whether or not you spend it. Each day you'll have to decide how you will invest that money in order to get the most enjoyment out of it. How would you approach that opportunity?

Guess what? You *already* have that opportunity. Every day, when you wake up and open your eyes, you have a bounty of riches to spend. Your account isn't full of money, though; it's full of time. No matter who you are—Richard Branson, Oprah Winfrey, or Joe Smith—you are given exactly the same amount of time as the next guy. Life doesn't care if you squander that time crying yourself silly at your computer or if you bask in the joy of every moment. Time passes just the same. Are you happy with how it's passing for you?

Although we may not have the ability to increase, slow down, or speed up time, we can choose how we spend it. After listening to story after story, what I learned from the FabFinders is that freedom of time is all about having more control over where and how your time is allocated.

Whether the FabFinders wanted to spend more time with their children, needed more time for leisure pursuits and hobbies, or just wanted more flexibility to decide when to work and when to play, time was a major driver of change. A law clerk's desire to play golf more often with her fiancé gave her the courage to tackle her shyness. A business consultant's dream to have time to travel around the world inspired his leap toward the land of entrepreneurship. The seasonality of a ski school eventually jump-started the school's owner to explore investing in real estate. The limitations of a 9-to-5 office job eventually led a graphic artist toward the flexibility of selling and flipping houses. For me, the amount of time I wasted on a daily basis responding to e-mails gave me reason enough to leave.

For Shelagh, time was the number one reason she chose to walk away from her life as a school teacher — what many would consider one of the most stable careers available. Although some may also think teachers have the most enviable working hours, Shelagh's story highlights just how important it is to have the freedom to plan those hours around your biggest priorities.

Shelagh's Story

Shelagh taught elementary school for eighteen years before she realized that other people's kids were getting more of her time and energy than her own children were. Although she enjoyed teaching, she didn't like having to compromise her role as a mom. Her desire to be there for her children was enough incentive to find a better way. Initially, she dabbled in tutoring, worked for a national training company, and tried her hand at blogging, but none of them completely fit her idea of fabulous. When she finally discovered how to parlay her master's degree in curriculum development and her teaching experience into something people needed, she found her true passion.

Acting as a consultant and business strategist, Shelagh now works with "mompreneurs," women who are mothers first and business owners second. "I love it. It's my passion, and it affords me the luxury of staying at home with my kids and still brings in some money," she says. Reflecting on her first few attempts to find another career, she explains how time was the key driver for change, but it was only part of the puzzle. The other jobs weren't really worth her time because they lacked the "passion piece."

The power of passion is evident in the success of her business: she currently makes more money consulting part-time than she did as a full-time teacher. Working mainly with other mothers, she can attest that time is the biggest challenge. Most of her clients have to juggle family time with the time required to run successful businesses. They often have to plan with their husbands so they don't have to go back to work while still bringing in a salary. Shelagh's ability to empathize with their situation makes her uniquely able to practice what she preaches.

Finally living a life that reflects her priorities, Shelagh tells me she had kids so she could enjoy them; her new business not only lets her do that, but also gives her the joy of helping other women do the same.

If Shelagh had listened to the sceptics or followed the status quo, she would still be struggling to accept the fact that her best time and energy was going to other people's kids. She is a great example of someone who dared to follow her desires and priorities toward finding her own version of fabulous. That's a lesson she couldn't teach her children from a classroom!

Consider the number of hours you work and who dictates when you work those hours. What would your life look and feel like if you could have more freedom with how you spend your time? Is the desire for that freedom enticing enough to get you started down the path to your best life?

Financial Freedom

Pay your bills, yes. But don't invest in them.
Invest in your dreams.

What you invest in grows.

Suzette Hinton

If that bank account I just offered you contained money instead of time, how much would it take to make you feel financially free? What if I told you that, in addition to that bank account, no one would ever ask you to pay for food or housing costs again? Would that change the amount you need to feel free? What if, instead of living in the US or Canada, you lived in a third world country, or, at the other end of the spectrum, somewhere with an extremely high cost of living? Would those things change the cost of your freedom? If you knew you'd have to pay medical bills for a loved one for ten or twenty years, or you'd end up raising six children, would that change the number?

Before I get too deep in examples, let me tell you a little secret I learned from the FabFinders: financial freedom has absolutely nothing to do with money. Okay, it has a little to do with it, but not as much as you might think. Financial freedom isn't about money; it's about choice. Just as we want to have control over our time, we want to have choice in our lives. If you ask me how much money I want to have, I'll tell you, "just enough." I want just enough to be able to do the kind of work I want, when I want. I want just enough to go the places I want to go and do the things I want to do.

I want enough to share my lifestyle with my friends and family, and enough that I will never have to think about "money" again. I don't need an excessive amount in order to do that, just enough. The amount to me is irrelevant!

Financial freedom means something different for everyone. If I didn't believe this before, the FabFinders certainly changed my viewpoint. Since I interviewed mostly successful professionals and corporate types, not many of them were financially constrained. However, several of them were still motivated to change as a result of finances. Having a surplus of money didn't seem to negate the desire for more freedom from it. Even those who were financially well-off wanted to be free to do what they wanted, go where they wanted, and be who they wanted to be. Those with big salaries felt trapped by the need to replace them at equally lucrative levels. Others who didn't have much money saw their lack of surplus as holding them back. Either way, the FabFinders saw their financial situations as chains that bound them.

Some dreamed of having the financial freedom for traveling and leisure pursuits. Others just wanted the freedom to break free from the stress of living paycheck-to-paycheck. Some wanted to make enough money to pay for a nanny so they could be free to go back to work, while others wanted the freedom to stay home and raise their children on their own. Whether financial freedom affords you the things you want and the ability to do things you love, or removes the stress and anxiety of things you don't, it can be a big motivator to transform your life.

Jess was so trapped in the reality of her financial situation that she didn't realize how much it was limiting her life. Not only had she stopped doing things she enjoyed, she had stopped dreaming about them. It seemed that accepting her situation made her lose sight of what was possible. That's when *possible* found her.

Jess' Story

> Jess' story is probably not that unique. Both she and her fiancé liked the work they did and believed they were fairly well paid for it. When they considered the vacations they could take, the things they could buy, and the life they wanted to have, they filtered it through the reality of how much

Chapter 1: Road to Freedom

they earned. However, they constantly struggled to pay their bills, and couldn't seem to save for their wedding. For Jess, not being able to pay for her wedding was the eye-opener to realizing that money was affecting the way she lived her life in general. For years, she just accepted that she would never be able to afford certain things. Then she had a change of perspective that transformed not only her bank account, but also her ability to dream.

It all started on the day Jess accompanied a friend to a spa party thrown by a network marketing company. The benefits of the all-natural products they sold proved to be the key to her new revelation. Initially, she just wanted a way to afford the products for her own use, but she began to consider the possibility of selling them herself. She was extremely shy, and she didn't think she had any talent for talking to people, let alone running her own business. However, the benefits of setting her own hours, building her own business, and getting to share an amazing product she believed in were too enticing.

As she describes it, "… they helped me learn to dream again. Before, I couldn't see a way out of my situation. They taught me about abundance and to see possibilities where I hadn't before."

At the time of the interview, Jess was building her new business, and she was able to go from full-time to part-time in her job as a law clerk. She credits this willingness for change to how much she has grown as a person throughout the process: "I was so influenced by others and my own self-limiting beliefs about money. Now I'm seeing the benefits as I push myself outside my comfort zone." Although she hasn't quite hit her goal of quitting her day job to pursue this endeavour full-time, she has found more balance in her life. The financial freedom that comes with her new passion means she is able to spend more time with her fiancé, and they can afford to go golfing and do other things they love. Incentives like that keep her motivated and pushing toward bigger and better goals.

I don't know that Jess' story is all that unique, and that's why I included it. How many of us are letting our ideas of "possible" hold us back from wanting more? How many of us assume that the amount of money we have gets to decide the kind of life we live? There is no guarantee that Jess will make millions of dollars in her new venture, or that she will ever be able to quit her day job, but who says she won't? I have to applaud not only her effort in going after her dreams, but also, more importantly, the shift that has taken place in her mind. It isn't hard to imagine that someone who refuses to let a small thing like money hold her back might be capable of making anything happen.

How about you? Do you wish you had more financial freedom in your life? How can you use that desire to inspire you to take a leap of faith toward new possibilities?

Freedom of Expression

Walk where your heart leads you, there are no restrictions and no burdens.

Gao Xingjian

Imagine for a moment, that shortly after you leave the confines of that room you were stuck in, you're invited to attend a party. It's going to be the event of the year, and it's rumoured to have the coolest guest list. That funny guy was invited—you know, the one who has that amazing talent to make everyone laugh. That sweet, kind girl will be there, and you know she is going to show up ready to make everyone feel comfortable and welcome. She'll probably bring along her cousin, the one who has that remarkable gift to make people feel important and relevant. That other guy might drop by—the extremely smart one who always seems to teach us some really bizarre but interesting facts about something we'd never normally think about. Everyone is expected to show up ready to share their amazing talent or gift with the rest of the group, and must come with their minds open to new ideas and acceptance of other's gifts. Can you imagine what it would be like to attend that party?

If you could be invited to a party like that, who would you be? What gifts would you choose to share with the group?

What if it wasn't just a party? What if your work life, your family life, or just life in general, was like that? What would the world look like if everyone felt free to express his or her true self? I don't know about you, but it sounds pretty fabulous to me. That's what I believe is at the heart of finding fabulous. Sure, it's partly about finding the ideal job or the perfect lifestyle and all that entails, but at the heart of it, Finding Fabulous is about finding *you*. In order to do that, you have to feel free to express who you truly are.

What does that mean? How do we do that in a world with all sorts of expectations and parameters about what's appropriate or ideal? How can we start to peel back the layers and wipe away years of societal pressures and self-limiting beliefs to find the heart of who we are?

At my former company, I had a bit of a reputation as having a big mouth. I love to talk, and quite loudly. I don't have much of a filter, and I express my opinions quite matter-of-factly. Love it or hate it, that's how I express myself. Whatever the issue, I like to dissect it down to the raw truth and tackle it at its core. As pragmatic as that approach may sound, it was becoming increasingly unacceptable during the downsizing of the company. As leadership changed hands and thousands of jobs were cut, exposing the real issues with frank discussions became a dangerous game.

During that time period, I struggled to know what was expected of me and struggled to figure out how I was supposed to act. If it wasn't safe to be me, who was I supposed to be? I didn't want to pretend to agree with decisions I felt were wrong. I didn't want to look away when something didn't feel right. I couldn't agree to stand behind information I didn't believe to be true. It just wasn't me. That's when I realized I felt trapped. I didn't feel free to be me.

Many of the FabFinders had similar issues with expressing their personalities in their past careers. A family counsellor struggled with the sombre atmosphere of teen angst and suicide. She longed to express her naturally spontaneous and carefree personality in an environment where she could laugh and have fun. Another woman spoke of feeling like she couldn't express her caring side in an impersonal office setting where no one really connected with each other.

At other times, the FabFinders found they couldn't express their integrity or values in a "back-stabbing" corporate culture, or in organizations that seemed to value the bottom line more than the quality of work they produced. A website designer spoke of feeling like she was "littering" the Internet with websites that didn't matter. A government worker spoke of the negative effects of underhanded office politics, both on the behaviour of those around him and on his own ability to make a positive difference.

Lack of autonomy was another way the FabFinders described being trapped by their circumstance. Although Tanya found success in the world of radio, it was the lack of control she had over what she produced that eventually turned her off of mainstream media.

Tanya's Story

"I climbed the corporate ladder only to realize it was leaning against the wrong wall," Tanya explains.

Despite being advised to avoid the world of journalism, Tanya devoted a great deal of her life to building a successful career in radio. Although she was a natural, and spent twenty-two years climbing the corporate ladder, she eventually became discouraged with the propaganda she was forced to produce. "I felt like my role in mainstream broadcasting was only helping to perpetuate fear and doubt," she explains.

It wasn't until her husband transferred to Europe, where she was unable to work, that she took the time for the introspection that would take her life in a completely different direction. It was the first time she had ever stopped to ask herself what she wanted and what kind of legacy she would leave. Following the concept that we become the company we keep and the thoughts we absorb, she began to wonder if she could offer a better alternative to mainstream media, and the idea for her radio station was born.

"We are influenced by the media in how we think, what we wear, how we look, and ultimately how we act," she says. Clarifying her purpose in life led her to discover her desire to deliver positive messages to the masses. Starting a web-based radio station that features only positive stories

and messages is her way of accomplishing that. She is committed to sharing positive stories from positive people that will inspire and motivate others to live full and happy lives. In the process, she found her own fabulous life, which includes the freedom to express her thoughts and beliefs on a regular basis.

Tanya wasn't the only FabFinder who felt "trapped" or confined by the processes of their company or the regulations of their industry. Like so many of us, she felt like she had little or no control over what prevented her from doing her highest-quality work. The crucial difference is that the FabFinders did something about it. Cutting the ties (in her case the gag order that prevented her from producing positive news), Tanya first had to walk away from the source of the problem. Then, impressively, she didn't wait around for the perfect job; she created it!

I wonder what more people would do if they knew that was possible. Do you long for more freedom of expression? What are you waiting for? Using Tanya's example for inspiration, what platform could you create to express *your* fabulous self?

Freedom to Change

> *We change our behaviour when the pain of staying the same becomes greater than the pain of changing. Consequences give us the pain that motivates us to change.*
>
> **Henry Cloud**

What all these ideas lead to, basically, is the freedom to change—our attitudes, our lives, and ourselves.

FabFinders spoke about eventually coming to a point when the feeling of being trapped or the longing for freedom trumped the fear of everything else. This point was key! They taught me many things, but one of the first was the power of clarity. Being clear about your motivation for change helps you change. Let's face it: change is hard! We need either really good reasons or really painful consequences to actually do it.

For me, once I internalized how it felt to live without the autonomy I desired, the ability to express myself, or the control over the quality I believed in, it started to actually feel more painful to go to work. Eventually, I moved beyond thinking and wishing for a better situation to a deep *need* for change. It built up over days and months, perhaps even years, and culminated in that moment in my kitchen when I knew it was time to go. That's the moment when I realized I couldn't be who I was meant to be if I stayed trapped by my circumstance. That realization sparked the decision; in turn, the decision caused me to act, and those actions became my journey.

How about you? Do you feel trapped or confined by your circumstances? Do you dream of more time or financial freedom? Do you yearn for more freedom to express yourself? Could that first step in the march toward freedom be the start of your journey to Finding Fabulous?

Roadmap: March Toward Freedom

Making a major career shift, or any similar life transformation, can be a scary, complicated endeavour. Everyone has different reasons for doing it, and usually many more for *not* doing it. The FabFinders demonstrated again and again how important it is to be clear on your "why." Understanding your own motivation can help break the inertia of staying the same; it will motivate you when things get tough and provide a filter for decisions you'll need to make along the way.

Consider your own situation and ask yourself the following questions:

☐ Do you feel trapped by your circumstances?

☐ Where would you like more freedom in your life?

- Does your work offer you the financial resources you need to live your definition of fabulous?

- Do you have the time to do the things that add to the foundation of your fabulous life?

- Is the time you have to spend on things you like (hobbies, passions, or even work-related tasks) in proportion to the time you spend on things you don't enjoy?

- Do you get to express your creativity while honouring your integrity and ability to deliver the quality you want?

Keeping your answers to the above questions close by, let's start to put them into perspective.

Not everyone needs a perfect scenario within all the parameters we've mentioned above. What's most relevant is how you feel about your situation and whether that prevents you from living the life you want to live.

Freedom of Time

Shelagh found herself spending all her energy and most of her time with other people's kids. Despite having the "ideal" working hours of a teacher, she realized it didn't fit with her biggest priority—spending time with her own family.

Everyone wishes they had more time, but consider:

- ☐ Do you feel trapped, either by the number of hours you work or the way those hours are scheduled?
- ☐ Does a lack of flexibility with your time prevent you from living the life you want to live?
- ☐ How would your life look and feel if you had more freedom to decide how you spend your time?
- ☐ Take the time to map out your ideal schedule.
  - ✓ Create a blank calendar (daily, weekly, or monthly, whichever makes most sense to you).
  - ✓ Create blocks of time for your biggest priorities and greatest desires.
  - ✓ Move those blocks of time around until you create your ideal schedule. Maybe you like to surf in the morning and start work at noon, or you want to work three days a week and play the other four. Whatever your ideal day looks like, put it in writing.
  - ✓ Don't limit yourself by what you think is realistic. Give your imagination *carte blanche* to brainstorm until you get a clear picture of what you want. We'll figure out the "how" later!

Financial Freedom

Jess had allowed her financial situation to dictate the type of life she was living. Not only did it stop her from doing things she wanted, it kept her from even dreaming about them! It's quite possible that you don't have all the financial resources you would like to have, but consider these questions:

- ☐ Are finances preventing you from living the life you want?
- ☐ Whether you make a lot of money or too little, reliance on a paycheck can feel very limiting. Is your paycheck keeping you in a job you hate?
- ☐ How would your life look and feel if you could gain more financial freedom?
- ☐ Make a list of all the things you would like to have, be, or do if money were no object.

    Review that list and ask yourself:

    - ✓ Do I feel trapped or confined by my current inability to have these things or experiences?
    - ✓ What small steps could I take today toward gaining more freedom where they are concerned?

Freedom of Expression

Both Tanya and I struggled in environments where we couldn't express ourselves. Tanya wanted to have a positive impact on mainstream media, and I wanted my opinions to matter. Not every situation is going to be a perfect fit. We both learned to find or create new environments that gave us the freedom to express our true selves.

- ☐ Do you feel your integrity is challenged by the tasks you're required to do for your job?
- ☐ Do you feel trapped by others dictating what defines quality work or service?
- ☐ How would your life look and feel if you had more freedom to express yourself at work?
- ☐ If you were invited to that party I mentioned, what person would the other guests see? How would you express yourself fully and authentically?

- ✓ Write out some of the key ways you express yourself when you feel you are really being *you*.
- ✓ Draw a picture (in your mind or on paper) of yourself, being you, at that party.

Motivation for Change

As you build a case and seek strong motivation for change, consider all of your answers to the questions above. As I mentioned, you don't necessarily have to have a vision of an all-encompassing, perfect scenario in order to start. Use your answers to guide your decisions and provide you with clues along the way.

If financial freedom is important to you, but not at the expense of creative expression, let that awareness guide your decisions. A cut in pay may be worth what you gain in job satisfaction, as long as the financial level isn't below a certain point.

Giving up some autonomy at work might be worth it if that gives you both the financial and time freedom you require to live the life you want. Just be sure that the lack of autonomy won't make you so unhappy that the extra time is spent in misery.

Chapter 2: Driven by Purpose

*Your purpose in life is to find your purpose
and give your whole heart and soul to it.*

Buddha

I'll never forget the feeling I had that day as I listened to the shocking, tragic events unfold on the radio. It was a beautiful September morning, and I was driving to Chatham, Ontario to meet with area urologists when the world seemed to spin out of control. Airplanes flying into buildings just didn't make any sense. Why? Who? What was happening? In an instant the whole world stopped and the meaning of everything seemed to shift. At the time, I was a pharmaceutical sales representative selling Viagra. Can you imagine how completely useless I felt that day, knowing my job was to engage physicians in a discussion about sexual dysfunction? How pointless was that?

A couple of weeks later, I spoke with a physician at an educational event for a cholesterol-lowering medicine. We shared our thoughts on 9/11— where we were when we heard the news and how we felt in those moments just after it happened. Irrelevant. That's how I felt that day: irrelevant. Guess what? So did he. He told me how he questioned what he did for a living and what it meant in the bigger picture. He spoke of how he just wanted to leave work, go home, and hug his family. I was stunned by his admission.

It made sense for *me* to feel that way; I was just a sales rep! But he saved lives every day; how could he possibly question the purpose in that?

Since then (and especially as I prepared to write this book), I often thought about that conversation as I struggled to understand my own purpose. However, it wasn't until I met the FabFinders that I started to fully comprehend what gives a particular role or job meaning and purpose. It used to be so easy to think that doctors, firemen, and police officers served the greatest purpose in our society, especially considering what they had to do during those days following 9/11. They save lives every day. What could have more purpose? But maybe it isn't so cut and dry as that.

What makes a particular job, position, or role purposeful? If you look up the definition in the dictionary, it literally means "having a useful reason for existing." Seems reasonable, but is that the only criteria? Who determines if something is "useful"?

In the case of the FabFinders, I learned very quickly that "useful" is in the heart of the beholder. There is no single formula or definition that fits everyone or every situation. My own bias was challenged as I listened to all kinds of interesting accounts of transformation, tales of individuals finding their purpose: stories like how a police officer longed to be a family doctor and how an occupational therapist's loss led to jewellery making. I heard from an autoworker who found a love for magic and an engineer who could "talk" to horses. The owner of an auto parts store found purpose in instructing golf; a teacher uncovered a creative way to reach struggling students. On the surface, one could debate whether their new roles serve a greater purpose than their last, but dive a little deeper, and you get to the heart of where purpose really lives.

If I've learned anything from the scores of interviews and hours of research, it has been the value of finding purpose within. Purpose is not something that inherently comes with a job title or a salary number. It's not a guarantee, and it's not universal. It is perhaps one of the few things that you can't find on Google.

Consider the examples I've already mentioned. Who has more purpose: a doctor or a police officer? Your answer might differ greatly, depending on

Chapter 2: Driven by Purpose

whether you are sick or being held at gunpoint. What about the auto parts owner versus the golf instructor? Again, if your car is falling apart the answer is quite obvious, but listen to the passion in one golf instructor's voice as she describes how self-confidence, trust, and integrity translate from the course to the boardroom (or even the operating room), and you might change your vote.

Maren was one of the FabFinders who challenged my understanding of this concept and taught me that meaning and purpose can be found in the most unlikely places.

Maren's Story

I could hear the passion and commitment in her voice as Maren explained that, at the age of thirteen, she knew she was destined to become an occupational therapist. It isn't hard to imagine how her kind, compassionate heart and desire to serve made her a valuable addition to the profession. However, despite years of working in that field, her faith would lead her down a different path, answering the call to provide therapy in a completely new and unexpected way.

If I told you, without the back-story, that Maren decided to give up being an occupational therapist in order to make jewellery, what would you think? Would you think she serves more or less purpose than before? How purposeful does accessorizing the world sound, compared to rehabilitating it?

Would it change your mind to learn that she found her new calling after her seven-year-old nephew died of a rare disease?

The spark of Maren's true purpose was lit a decade after her nephew's death. As Maren and his mother were reminiscing and grieving the ten-year anniversary of their loss, her sister opened a chest that held the few mementos she had of his life. She remarked how she wished she had a handprint to remember him by.

On a mission to ease her sister's grief and commemorate her nephew, Maren went to work on a special silver charm. She soon realized how much comfort and peace people could gain from such a small symbol, d she knew she had found her purpose. Combining her natural artistic talents with the compassion of someone who knows the pain of loss, Maren now creates lasting memories through jewellery. Stamping thumb, hand, foot, and even paw prints into silver, she is able to give people a lasting impression of their loved ones. Far beyond the value of the jewellery itself, she provides a different kind of therapy that helps to ease the pain of loss. Speak to any of her clients and I'm sure you will understand the purpose in that!

Now that you know the back-story, I'll ask you again, "Does being a therapist serve a greater purpose than making jewellery? Maren's story highlights how *why* we do something can be much more important that *what* we do. After meeting Maren, I now *know* that purpose is in the heart of the beholder. It doesn't matter if someone else feels like you are serving a significant purpose; you have to feel that for yourself. Get over thinking that purpose is related to hierarchy, title, or salary grade, and know that it's more important for it to align with your values, desires, and beliefs.

Hearing firsthand how disengaged individuals became with their roles, I can imagine how that impacts the purpose they are able to serve. A disengaged police officer could miss a critical sign or misread criminal behavior. A disengaged doctor could prescribe the wrong medicine or misdiagnose a condition. A disengaged teacher might fail to inspire and engage her students. All of the seemingly purposeful roles suddenly lack meaning when seen through the eyes of someone who isn't aligned to that purpose.

Understanding what you have to offer the world, and listening to what feels right, allows you to align your purpose to whatever role or job you choose. How do you spend the majority of the day? What purpose are you serving? Does it align with your values and ring true to your heart?

Defining Purpose

> *The purpose of life is not to be happy. It is to be useful, to be honorable, to be compassionate, to have it make some difference that you have lived and lived well.*
>
> **Ralph Waldo Emerson**

In some form or other, the FabFinders talked about needing to make a difference. Whether or not they personally longed for more freedom, there was a subset who spoke passionately about wanting to serve the world in a meaningful way. This was their key driver for change. Some held the firm belief that we are meant to serve a particular purpose, like the former chiropractor who discovered her true purpose through years of intense meditation, or the program director who told me he felt called by God to serve the needs of children. Even those who didn't identify or agree with having a particular purpose still spoke of an increased connection with their work that reeked of purpose-driven ambition. A former factory worker told me he just wanted to feel more connected to what he was doing, while a new entrepreneur wanted to leave something behind for her children.

Overt awareness aside, it became abundantly clear that, as a group, the FabFinders had a primitive need to matter. In terms of their motivation to change, the FabFinders defined their desire for more purpose in one of three ways:

SPIRITUAL PATH – these individuals believe that God, or the universe, has a particular plan for them. Some of them have known about that purpose for years, while others have just recently come to realize it. They are striving to gain clarity so they can live the purpose they were put on this Earth to fulfill.

LASTING LEGACY – these individuals don't necessarily believe they were meant to fulfill a particular purpose, but they long to leave a lasting legacy. They want to know that after they are long gone, what they did with their time mattered.

CARING CONNECTION – these individuals are more concerned with connecting to what they do for a living. They don't necessarily buy into living a particular purpose, but they want to be more interested and invested in what they do. In essence, they want what they do to matter to them.

The intention of this book is not to decide whether everyone has a "God-given" purpose, or to even suppose everyone must go out and find one particular purpose in order to feel fulfilled. The stories and concepts presented in this chapter are merely meant to challenge you to think about the role of purpose in your journey of Finding Fabulous.

Does searching for purpose in one of the three described ways feel right for you? If so, how could you use that desire to get you started down the path to finding it?

Pathways to Purpose

It is not enough to be industrious; so are the ants.
What are you industrious about?

Henry David Thoreau

As I sat atop my suitcase, staring down the empty road and willing the bus to arrive, I kept thinking, "There must be a better way." How was it possible that the journey from the airport to our hotel was taking us longer than the flight from Detroit to Denver?

I had arrived in Colorado with two friends (fellow graduate students) to attend an international conference. Even though, like them, I was on a tight student budget, I wanted to share a cab, thinking the convenience would be worth any extra cost. However, I was overruled by my much thriftier friend, and we ended up on a journey reminiscent of Steve Martin and John Candy's movie *Planes, Trains, & Automobiles*.

The airport shuttle brought us to the downtown area, where a free trolley carted us a mile or so up the street to wait for the city bus that would eventually take us to our hotel. Unfortunately, it was a holiday, and the city bus only ran on the hour. Judging by the length of time we had been waiting, we had obviously just missed it.

Why did this have to be so difficult? Surely it was worth a couple of extra bucks to avoid lugging those heavy suitcases up and down the steps of each vehicle and to keep us from losing our entire first day in Denver. Despite the patience I had to muster up on the street corner that day, I think the experience taught me something valuable, a lesson that was reinforced five days later on the return trip home. Deciding not to leave my fate in the hands of my friend again, I did some research and found a rental car for less than the cost of our collective bus tickets. We had the car the entire day before we left to go sightseeing, got ourselves a fast and convenient trip to the airport, and saved money to boot!

So what's the lesson? There are many pathways to get you from point A to point B, some more fun than others. Taking the time to do a little research, or at the very least ask some basic questions, can save you a lot of time and frustration. In addition, the mere awareness that a trip might be long and challenging helps you better prepare for it. Had I known that trip into Denver was going to take so long, I'd have picked another option, or at least planned how to spend time between bus rides.

The path to finding purpose isn't all that different. For years, I kept waiting to figure out what I was meant to do. I would often say, "When I know what I want to be, I'll become it." In a way, I was sitting at a corner of my life, willing that bus of purpose to drive by and pick me up! Had I known I was going to have to do a lot of work and introspection to figure out what I was meant to do before I could do it, I'd have started sooner. Perhaps if I had known my purpose wasn't on the same route or guaranteed to arrive at a set time, I wouldn't have waited so long for it to come around. Maybe knowing the process would be challenging and frustrating would have helped me learn to relax and enjoy the ride.

Listening to the various ways the FabFinders found their purpose, I came to further appreciate this idea of different pathways. There were "ah-ha" moments from teachers, coaches, and speakers as they remembered playing schoolhouse or presenting in front of their teddy bears when they were young. Sometimes there was an extreme wake-up call, like the brain bleed that instigated a credit manager's transformation to become a personal fitness trainer. Other times it was subtle, like the deep, gut-level desire a pharmaceutical representative felt to make a bigger impact on the healthcare system. And perhaps not quite as often, there were those whose knowing came straight out of the blue, like the entertainer who couldn't bear the idea of working the line in a factory for the next thirty years.

Have you always known what gifts you offer the world, or are you still trying to figure it out? Can you think of a favourite game or toy from your childhood that might give you clues to the purpose you are meant to serve? Have you maybe just stumbled onto to something that feels really meaningful, something you can leave as a legacy? Clearly everyone has a different path for finding more purpose in their work and their lives in general. There is no right or wrong way, only the way that presents to you.

As I reflect back on the interviews, it seems the FabFinders' paths to finding purpose could be described one of five ways:

- **Born to Know**
- **Signs from Youth**
- **Jolted to Discovery**
- **Seekers**
- **Finders**

Taking time to understand and, perhaps more importantly, accept your own path can help you better plan for the journey that lies ahead. The awareness is quite empowering. Instead of waiting around like I did, it allows you to start taking action toward finding and eventually living your purpose.

Review each of the different paths and consider if any resonate with you. How does understanding your path to purpose change your journey?

Born to Know

> *I grew up thinking I could be an artist,*
> *but I've been one since I was born.*
>
> **Unknown Author**

I've always been envious of the lucky ones—you know, the ones who were born ready to take on the world with their gifts and talents, the ones who didn't have to read six hundred self-help books to figure it out. They weren't sitting at that corner with me, waiting for the bus of purpose to come by; they were on the train, the fast track to their fabulous. They were the ones who always seemed to know what they wanted to do with their lives, and always seemed to be able to pursue it with passion and intention. I think of people like country music star Taylor Swift and professional golfer Tiger Woods. Considering that Taylor's talent and love for singing started when she was nine years old, and she was writing songs by the age of twelve, I'd say she is one of the lucky ones. As for Tiger, what was he, about two when his golf prowess appeared?

I'm a firm believer that everyone has a special, unique talent, whether they know it or not, and whether they choose to use it or not. But I have to say, there is something magical about a purpose so strong and pure that it presents in the form of a toddler! Think about the "head start" Taylor and Tiger got on the rest of us. Imagine what could have been possible for your own life if you had started working toward your life's purpose before you even reached puberty.

Although I'm not sure what age Cathy was when her passion started to take form, she is another of the lucky ones who had an enviable clarity of purpose. However, as you will learn from her story, just because someone may have always known his or her purpose doesn't necessarily mean they always follow it.

Cathy's Story

All the girls would line up at her door before parties and events to have her make them something new or alter what they already had. I always wondered how she got her course work done with all that sewing going on. It wasn't necessary to know Cathy very long before you understood this was a deep passion, and, fortunately for her, also a great talent.

Uniquely, her small dorm room was stuffed full of sewing machines, material scraps, customized clothing patterns, and various other tools I couldn't begin to name. Can you guess what she was studying at university? Political science. What? Why on earth would she waste her time and talent getting a basic degree that seemed to serve little purpose for her inevitable career path? The answer was probably not that surprising or unique: since her father was paying for her education, she had to complete a basic degree before she was allowed to pursue her passion.

Why? What did her parents say when, as a young child, she proclaimed she would one day be a famous fashion designer? Did they applaud her make-believe fashion shows and smile encouragingly at the whims of their young child? At what point did they think she couldn't make a living doing that, or at least doubt it enough to feel she needed a degree to "fall back on"?

Unfortunately, I lost contact with Cathy after I left university, so I'm not sure if she was ever able to realize her dream. Did she ever go to school for fashion design? Was she able to make a career of it? Does she still love it as much as she did back then?

Perhaps it was my envy of her singular, clear purpose which made it hard for me to understand what Cathy was waiting for. I'd have given anything to have that much conviction of purpose. Whether or not Cathy chose to make a living with her passion or kept it for a hobby is beside the point. I'm more interested to know if she honoured that sense of purpose by using her gifts in a way that added joy and happiness to her life.

Since this book is all about major career transformations, it's probably not that surprising to find that I didn't interview many FabFinders who were born knowing what purpose they were meant to serve. Sure, some of them had inclinations or retrospectively connected the dots of their lives, but none of them recalled knowing all along, without a doubt. Nonetheless, I think this path to purpose warrants mentioning, especially for those of you struggling to live the purpose you were born to live.

If you are one of the "lucky ones," the question for you is simple: are you living the purpose you were born to live? How could you leverage your passions and talents to serve an even greater purpose?

Signs from Youth

Although not everyone is lucky enough to have been born knowing their purpose, it was interesting to hear the stories of some FabFinders who had clues from their childhood. Some of them quite blatantly pointed it out for me; others mentioned it so subtly I had to wonder if they themselves made the connection. I asked several of them what game or toy they loved most as a child, and I wasn't totally surprised when the answers seemed to be somewhat related to their "newly discovered" purpose or passion. I heard how a bank teller who later became a writing professor used to spend her days making up stories. She mentioned how her mother would worry that she spent too much time in her imagination instead of the real world. Another lady explained how she would line up her teddy bears so she could present to them. At the time of the interview, she had traded in her corporate career in commercial real estate marketing to become a seminar leader and inspirational speaker.

The topic of finding and living your purpose is an important one, and perhaps seems more complicated than my reference to the whims and games of a young child. However, regardless of how long it took or how winding the road was that led to *Finding Fabulous*, there was often a connection.

In Maria's case, the joys from her childhood seemed to sneak back into her life when she wasn't looking.

Maria's Story

> "It felt excruciating. I was totally uninterested," she says, explaining how she felt about the course work she endured to obtain her degree in mechanical engineering. So why did she do it? What purpose was served by her suffering?

As a child, Maria had always been quite creative, demonstrating an early talent for drawing. However, in addition to her love for and skill with the arts, she was also very good at math and science. Since she was raised with the belief that artistic fields should be left for girls who didn't perform well in those subjects, she went with the flow and followed the advice to go into engineering. It made sense to her at the time, since her father's own artistic and musical talents were things he did on the side, not as an actual career.

However, it didn't take long for Maria to become completely disinterested in her major. Whenever possible, she selected courses with more of a creative aspect, like industrial or graphic design. Given her disinterest, it wasn't too surprising that she left the profession behind when she took a hiatus to raise her children. Occasionally, while she was home with her kids, she would be asked to do some technical drawings; when a few of those clients started asking her to do some more creative designs, she began to rediscover the passion from her youth.

Even though she enjoyed the creative nature of the work, she surprised herself with her ability to do it. In an effort to further explore this aspect of herself which she had given up on as a child, she signed up for a fine arts class. Although she wasn't interested in pursuing fine arts, it was enough validation, as her teacher suggested, that she had talent.

Eventually that confidence led Maria to graphic design, and she started working for a company developing print ads for magazines. When that company went under, she opened a business with another partner. Taking most of the clients with them, they were able to run a successful graphic design and marketing company for nearly fifteen years. Although the partners eventually went their separate ways, in the end Maria was able to combine what she always loved to do as a child (creative design) with what she became really good at (technical design) in order to fulfill her purpose. As she describes the creative work she does for her clients today, I see the sparkle in her eyes—the sparkle of a young child who finally gave herself permission to do what she loves to do!

Even though Maria stumbled upon her passion and purpose almost accidentally, I started to wonder if this wasn't a strategic approach that the rest of us could take intentionally. For those of us struggling to find our purpose, maybe we could venture back to the carefree days of our youth to find some clues. Thinking back to my own childhood, my favourite toy was Lego. I loved the ability to create something new from the basic building blocks. It was like getting a new toy each and every time you opened up the box! Did my desire to be creative and to build a company of my own start many years ago on the living room carpet? All those plays I used to write and perform for my mom: were they clues to a career in writing or speaking?

What toy or game do you remember most fondly from your childhood? Could that provide clues to your passions and help uncover your intended purpose?

Jolted to Discovery

Sometimes the path to discovering your purpose can be painful. I don't mean waiting-for-a-bus-on-a-holiday painful, I mean literally painful! Some of the FabFinders didn't choose to go on a particular mission to find meaning or purpose. Some of them were perfectly happy, or so they thought. Then some major event or incident happened that opened their eyes, turned their lives upside down, and led them down the path to discovering their purpose. Often it was traumatic, like a car accident or a brain bleed. Sometimes it was just an awakening as a result of an event, like a divorce or birth of a child, that made them re-evaluate what they were doing and why.

For Sandra, it was more like a "smack upside the head" that finally woke her up to a new purpose.

Sandra's Story

It didn't occur to her that something was terribly wrong. Waking up with a monstrous, migraine-like headache wasn't enough to slow down this hardworking, ambitious professional. The signs were there: she was unable to button her blouse, she was exhausted all the time, and she felt like she was driving in a fog, but these red flags still didn't convince her to seek treatment. It wasn't until five days later, when her speech was altered and she stumbled into a doorframe, that Sandra finally went to her doctor. Although her physician initially thought she might have a brain tumour, an out-of-town trip to the closest neurosurgeon clarified that Sandra had a life-threatening brain bleed.

Since the surgery to fix the bleed was also life-threatening, the doctors decided to admit her to hospital and hope the medications would reduce the swelling and cause the brain to reabsorb the bleed. Over the next several days, her symptoms worsened as she lost the ability to walk or lift her arm. It would be another five days before her symptoms started to dissipate and she was released to recover at home.

Grateful, but knowing there must be a lesson in the experience, she worked hard to figure out what her life was trying to tell her. Why, at the young age of forty-eight, was this happening? What did it all mean? What was she supposed to do with her life?

One day, she repeatedly wrote the words "speak, teach, and train" on a piece of paper. These were things she loved to do, and she felt they had some connection with her future. She had worked for thirty years as a successful credit manager, and it never occurred to her to do anything else. And yet, days after she wrote down those three words, she awakened with an "ah-ha" moment. For years, she had felt a strong passion for fitness, and many people had suggested that she turn that passion into a business. Finally, that idea felt right.

With a clear picture and a new plan in place, Sandra figured she could start building her expertise and get her business ready in her spare time as she returned to the corporate world. She resumed her previous position with newfound insight, and she quickly began to understand how the stress and workload of her job had played a role in her illness. At the same time, the company was changing around her: she found she had less autonomy, and it seemed her expertise was not as valued as it had been. It was as if her life was speaking to her again. All the things she loved about her job were starting to change, and there were signs everywhere that it was a great time to leave. Just over a year later, she finally left her corporate job and opened her personal training business full-time.

One of the most surprising comments Sandra made during our interview was how she realized that being sick was one of the happiest times of her life. There was a sort of euphoria she felt about simply being alive, along with a greater sense of gratitude that can only come from experiencing a life-threatening situation. She had a fresh perspective, understanding what life looked like without all the pressure and stress that came with her job. She started to appreciate things she had once hated, like cooking. Finding the time to learn and do different things made them more enjoyable. She had been happy with her previous success, so she had never stopped to think about what other things she might be missing. Now she defines success differently, and she's learning what it's like to live with purpose.

For me, Sandra's story isn't about waiting for the life-threatening, life-altering moments to live on purpose. It's more a heads-up or a warning not to wait. However, for those people who experience major events that change their perspective, the message is, "So what are you going to do about it?" Don't let the event be in vain.

What is your life telling you? How will you honour the lessons your life is teaching you and start to live with more purpose?

Seekers

There are times to stay put, and what you want will come to you, and there are times to go out into the world and find such a thing for yourself.

Lemony Snicket

Those of us who don't have the good fortune to be born knowing what we want to do, or to have passions stirred up from our childhoods, must do a little more work to find our purpose. These include the FabFinders who, like me, proactively went looking for answers and did a lot of self-growth exercises to uncover their purpose. Many of the life coaches I spoke to seemed to stumble upon their new career paths when they sought out coaches for themselves. One sales representative found her purpose as she searched for an answer to some of the issues that frustrated her about her industry. After attending a coaching session to figure out her own potential, a marketing executive stumbled upon her life's purpose: to help other women discover theirs.

Often these "seekers" spoke of how uncomfortable their lives had gotten prior to their journeys. Unlike the "jolted to discovery" people, the realization and the need to find purpose crept up on them more slowly, after years of subconsciously knowing that something wasn't quite right. A fitness trainer recalled the constant sense that he was meant to do *something* greater than what he was doing, even though he didn't completely know what that something was. It took being fired from a few jobs, years of personal growth, and starting his own company before he found that greater calling. For another FabFinder, an HR director, it took years of voracious journaling to uncover his purpose.

Tania was another of those FabFinders I call a Seeker. Geographically speaking, she may have traveled the furthest in her exploration of who she really is and what purpose she is here to serve.

Tania's Story

When the travel bug bit Tania five years ago, she couldn't imagine how far it would take her, or how much she would grow personally, before it led her back home again. At the time, she was working as a sales representative for a large pharmaceutical company in Canada. The desire to travel internationally, experience new cultures, and meet new people resulted in her decision to apply for an MBA program in Barcelona. In addition to living in Spain, that experience took her to Switzerland and China, where she met people from all over the world and learned a lot about herself. After graduation, she accepted a marketing position with a health care company out of Zurich.

Even though the job seemed to fit the criteria she was looking for, it was draining all of her energy, had her feeling "out of whack," and she found herself emotionally exhausted. At one point she spoke of having a sort of out-of-body experience, not recognizing herself. Knowing things wouldn't change unless she did something, she followed a friend's advice and attended a seminar for life coaches in London. The experience gave her more insight than she expected: it led to a five-month coaching course in Norway and the inevitable resignation from her company.

Before jumping into her new coaching career, Tania wanted to learn more about what she wanted out of life. Her search led to the trip of a lifetime, a 177-day journey that crossed four continents and passed through seventeen countries. Although some people thought she was taking an extended vacation (or simply escaping her life), her adventure took on a deeper meaning, providing fresh insight and guidance for her future.

Reflecting on the trip, she believes it was all about connection. Not only did she connect with strangers and friends, she also connected more with herself than she ever thought possible. It gave her incredible clarity about what she values, what brings her energy, and what she feels is her life's purpose.

Packing her bags along with her newfound insight, Tania went back home to Canada, where she launched her coaching business. Her goal is to help her clients amplify their impact and find ways to connect with themselves and others. Although Tania's journey of self-discovery, and her world adventures, are far from over, she's already found a pretty fabulous life!

I don't think we need to take a six-month trip around the world to find ourselves or discover our purpose. However, I do believe that many of us have to travel outside our comfort zones to discover something new about ourselves. Whether that means learning a new skill, taking on a new responsibility, meeting new people, or just studying our own thoughts and feelings, it requires action.

Are you struggling to discover your purpose in life? If so, what are you doing about it? What action could you take today to bring you one step closer?

Finders

My sister once said to me, "I don't have the same desire as other people to go find my purpose or be more fulfilled." She said it in a sort of resigned, "Is there something wrong with me?" kind of way. Considering that she's an elementary school teacher who lights up whenever she talks about her students and their progress, I found it kind of funny. Given the energy and enthusiasm she devotes to her profession, I'd say she's already found her purpose. She doesn't have to go out and search for it.

Almost as enviable as the "born to know" group, the "finders" weren't intentionally looking for their purpose. Often they spoke about the happenstance of their lives and identified the breadcrumbs of various experiences that led them to their purpose.

Janel is a good example of what I call a "finder." Although she wasn't particularly happy with what she was doing, her purpose seemed to gallop up beside her when she wasn't looking.

Janel's Story

Not entirely sure what her college major should be, Janel listened to her guidance counsellor, who referred to engineering as "the passport to the world." Since she was naturally gifted in math and science, a degree in mechanical engineering seemed a logical choice.

After school and a few contract jobs, Janel accepted a position at an energy auditing firm, where she was responsible for estimating and sizing rooftop heating and cooling systems. Everyone around her was passionate about geothermal systems, yet she felt like she was doing calculations all day for something she didn't really understand, much less like.

Around this time, Janel's sister got her back into something she had loved long before: riding, and eventually owning, horses. The first horse she bought was quite wild and difficult to handle. Accepting an offer from the owner of the barn, Janel witnessed the power of Equine Bowen, a holistic, soft-tissue therapy aimed at stimulating the body's ability to heal itself. Within three weeks, and after only three sessions, Janel's horse had an amazing breakthrough.

Fascinated by the results, and hoping to save money by performing the treatments herself, she decided to learn the technique. She didn't intend to make a business out of it, but she couldn't deny how well the horses responded to her and how much joy it brought her.

Although she admits it was quite a leap from the scientific, "black and white" background of engineering to the more natural, intuitive approach of Equine Bowen, she can appreciate the advantages her education brings to her work with horses. As an Equine Bowen therapist, she had to learn to listen to the horse and wait for it to "speak" to her. The basic fundamentals and problem-solving skills she used in mechanical engineering have helped her become a better horse therapist and opened her up to a whole new way of looking at life.

She refers to the "cookie crumbs" of her life that brought her to this place. She doesn't see her time as an engineer as wasted; instead, she views it as a step toward developing her passions and purpose in life. Who knew that a mechanical engineer could become a horse whisperer?

Although she didn't have to spend years writing in a journal or taking self-help seminars to find her purpose, I do believe Janel did one critical thing in finding her purpose; she followed her passion. Riding horses had always been a passion of hers; she had just stepped away from it for a few years. Her example is an important one. Whether or not you believe you are here to fulfill one particular purpose, follow your passions. Do things you love to do. Be with people, animals, or things you love to be with. Go to places, events, or environments that make you happy and inspire you. If you truly are a "finder," your purpose just might gallop up beside you like Janel's did.

Are you setting yourself up for success? What could you do to follow your passions and bring yourself closer to your purpose?

The intention of this book is not to uncover your purpose. There are several books, experts, coaches, and seminars to help you with that. The aim of this section is to explore the idea of living purposefully, and how that intention can be a powerful motivator of change. The FabFinders' examples merely illustrate what is possible while offering some guideposts for others who wish to do the same. Just as you will need to do, they had to forge their own unique paths to finding and living their purpose.

Roadmap: Design a Path of Purpose

The path of *Finding Fabulous* isn't always easy, and it isn't something everyone wants, or even needs, to follow. The steps outlined below are meant to help you discover if you want to live more purposefully, and dare you to consider what impact that could have on your life.

What does living purposefully mean to you?

Ask yourself the following questions to clarify which of the three reasons for wanting more purpose resonate with you most:

Spiritual Path *(thoughts or belief that God or the Universe has a bigger plan for you)*

- ☐ Are you looking to uncover the bigger plan for your life?
- ☐ Do you believe you are supposed to serve a particular purpose? If so, do you know what it is?

Leaving a Legacy *(the desire to leave your mark on the world, or to leave something behind for others)*

- ☐ Are you interested in leaving a legacy behind?
- ☐ Do you wonder if, once you are gone, whether what you did will matter to anyone?

Caring Connection *(a longing to be more interested or invested in what you do on a daily basis)*

- ☐ Are you looking to find a deeper meaning or connection with what you do?
- ☐ Do you believe it is possible to love what you do for a living?

Keep your answers to the above questions close by as you start down your path to finding and living your purpose. Refer to them any time you are discouraged, frustrated, or feeling anxious to remind yourself why you are doing this.

How is purpose showing up in your life?

As you consider your journey of finding purpose, remember the image of me sitting atop that suitcase, willing that bus to drive down the road. I stayed in a job for years, believing my "purpose" would just magically drive by and pick me up. The FabFinders taught me that purpose comes down different roads and arrives at different times, so we must be willing to notice when and how ours arrives.

Consider the various paths and think about which one resonates most with your life experiences.

- Born to Know
- Signs from Youth
- Jolted to Discovery
- Seeker
- Finder

Born to Know

Cathy was born with a talent and love for sewing, but she was pursuing a backup plan when I met her. Think about the passions you have always felt and how they fit into the purpose you are meant to live.

- ☐ Have you always known, but not acted upon, your purpose?
- ☐ Why haven't you acted until now?
- ☐ How will your life change if you choose to act now?

If this path of finding purpose resonates with your experience:

- ☐ Write down all the excuses you've made that have kept you from living your dream. Beside each excuse:
  - ✓ Write one reason that excuse isn't true.
  - ✓ Write one thing you could do this week to counteract it.

Signs from Youth

Maria didn't realize that her childhood love of drawing would someday become tied to her purpose. It's possible the answers to your questions about your purpose lie somewhere in your past. Don't overlook the power and purity of childhood wishes and dreams.

- ☐ What game or toy did you most enjoy as a child?
- ☐ Was there some skill or talent you had as a child that you might have been directed away from because it wasn't a "realistic" career choice?
- ☐ How will your life change if you start doing more of the things you used to enjoy in the carefree days of your youth?

If this path of finding purpose resonates with your experience:

- ☐ Make a list of things you can start doing that you used to love or that correspond to the game or toy you mentioned (i.e., find adult versions of those childhood games).
  - ✓ Look for other possibilities to bring those elements into your current work or life situation.

Jolted to Discovery

Sandra got a huge wake-up call when a life-threatening brain bleed forced her to stop and re-evaluate her life. Regardless of what incident may have happened to you, consider whether it could serve as a lesson or "heads up" to your intended purpose.

- ☐ Did some event or situation happen to change your perspective or open your eyes to new possibilities?
- ☐ What was the change, and what does it mean for your current situation?
- ☐ How will your life change if you act on the lessons of that situation?

If this path of finding purpose resonates with your experience:

- ✓ Write out the lessons you have learned from the experience (either in a list form or journal entries).
- ✓ Brainstorm some specific ways you could implement changes associated with what you've learned (e.g., if you spend too many hours at work, pre-schedule down time; if you took someone for granted, plan activities with them; if you can't find meaning in your work, explore new options).

Seeker

You don't have to take a six-month journey across the world to find your purpose the way Tania did, but taking *some* type of action may get you to your destination faster.

- ☐ Do you long to do something else, but you don't know what?
- ☐ How could your life be different if you make a decision to find the answers to your questions?
- ☐ What steps could you take today to live more purposefully?

If this path of finding purpose resonates with your experience:

- ☐ Stop waiting for your purpose to magically appear. Take actions that will give you new perspective on your possibilities. You could:
    - ✓ Read books
    - ✓ Take a course
    - ✓ Journal your feelings
    - ✓ Find new role models

Finder

Janel wasn't actively looking to find a new purpose, but following her passion for horses helped her stumble upon it.

- ☐ Did you just sort of stumble upon your purpose?
- ☐ Are you happy with your situation, or are there things you'd like to change?
- ☐ How can your life be different if you find even better ways to live that purpose?

If this path to finding purpose resonates with your experience:

- ✓ Develop a "super-state" of awareness so you can continue to follow the signs that lead to your dreams as they evolve over time.
- ✓ Continue following your passions and do things that bring you joy!

Section II: Potholes & Pitfalls

When eating an elephant, take one bite at a time.

Creighton Abrams

"It's so easy for you!" she huffed between laboured breaths, sweat dripping down her face as I clapped and cheered her into camp. Easy? What? That day had been many things, but easy was not one of them. Just like the sixty-three-year-old woman standing in front of me, I too had spent the day gasping for air as I navigated the four thousand-foot ascent toward *Dead Woman's Path* on the Inca Trail. Even though I had trained for months and I was in the best shape of my life, the entire time I was thinking, "I'm so out of shape!" The high altitude and steep stone steps of the trail were pushing more than my lung capacity; they were pushing my limits! With each step, I negotiated how many more I could climb before I would allow myself to rest. Approaching the summit, that number had dwindled to only one or two. How could she possibly think it had been easy for me?

As I considered her comments, standing there looking out over the Peruvian landscape, I had a little epiphany: easy isn't something you can assess for someone else. Even if it were, where would it get you? After all, my hiking mate and I were standing in the exact same location. We had both taken the exact same trail. We had both given it our all, placed one foot in front of the other, and reached our destination. Sure, I may have entered camp a few hours ahead of her, but she still made it. Why did she think this was *easier* for me? Why did it even matter?

Since that conversation, and throughout the process of writing this book, I've become super-sensitive to the word *easier*. It seems people love to toss it out as a reason or excuse for not taking action. I'd hear people say it was *easier* for me to follow my dreams because I didn't have kids. Then I'd meet a single mom of five who succeeded in creating her own business. Or someone would say it was *easier* for younger people to start over or learn new things. Then I'd hear about an eighty-nine-year-old woman who was learning to blog and selling products online. Others might say it was *easier* for someone with lots of money or people who lived in a prosperous urban center, because they had more options. But then I'd read about a man who overcame a mountain of debt and created a location-independent business, despite living on a fairly isolated island and having zero experience.

Easier is not only impossible to decipher for someone else, it is also a trap! Get stuck assessing what is *easier* for other people, and you waste valuable time and energy that could be spent on determining what's *possible* for you. That's what this section is all about.

When I started doing interviews, I didn't really care what was or wasn't easy for people. I didn't care if they were younger or older, or if they were richer or poorer than me. It didn't matter if they had more resources or the best connections. I just wanted the inside scoop. What could I expect? What potholes and pitfalls could I prepare for? Was there a simpler solution or straighter path than the one I was taking? How could they help pave the bumpy, winding road I had started walking down?

The following chapters highlight the four biggest challenges revealed in the interviews. Rather than focusing on what was easy and what wasn't, we will discuss how the FabFinders overcame their biggest issues. Like the FabFinders, you may not experience all of the pitfalls mentioned here, but these four were the most prevalent amongst the group—the most common objections, reasons, and excuses I heard from others stuck in miserable jobs and situations.

Biggest Challenges:

- **You**
- **Money**
- **Support**
- **Environment**

Whether their paths led them around, over, under, or even through their barriers, the FabFinders' examples offer some inspired ideas and suggestions. The intention of this section isn't to provide you with the solutions to all of your challenges; I honestly feel those are already inside of you. However, I do believe the footsteps of those who have gone before us can smooth the path. By demystifying the magnitude of the problem in the first place, their solutions often seemed too simple and too obvious; maybe that new perspective is the greatest gift of all. When they break down the biggest barriers into manageable chunks, perhaps they help us "eat the elephant, one bite at a time."

Regardless, I hope that at the very least this section will dare you to reconsider what you are allowing to get in your way of *Finding Fabulous*.

What is currently holding you back?

What is your biggest barrier?

What could your life look and feel like if you overcome your barriers?

Chapter 3: You

*What great thing would you attempt
if you knew you could not fail?*

Robert H. Schuller

Can you imagine if life was like "Who Wants to be a Millionaire?"— a game whose intended goal is obvious and straightforward, with built-in fail-safes along the way? Wouldn't that be cool? If life was actually like that, what would you be willing to risk to capture the big prize?

For those of you who aren't familiar with this American television game show, contestants are required to answer increasingly difficult trivia questions in the pursuit of a million dollars. For each question they answer correctly, their pot of money grows. The only caveat: at each new level they must risk the amount of money they've already won in the attempt to win more. However, the best part is that each contestant is given three "lifelines" to help them when they get stuck. When all the lifelines are used up, the players are on their own.

As I consider all the tough decisions I've had to make over the past several years, I become quite envious of those odds. Can you imagine what would be possible if you could have three lifelines during your transformation? My imagination runs wild as I start to picture how much brighter and bolder

I could be. In my version, the "call a friend" lifeline would be a game-changer: I'd allow that "friend" to come from the future, and I could even call my future self to ask her what decision would be best. I'd reverse the "ask the audience" lifeline to be a sort of "ask the experts," only I'd make myself the expert. That way, anything I say or do would be accepted because I'd have the credibility I needed. Then I'd change the "50/50" lifeline to a "do-over," so anytime I chose the wrong option I could rewind time and pick the right one. Wouldn't that be awesome?

What about you? If you could create your own categories of lifelines to ensure you found the work and life you wanted, what would you choose? Armed with those secret weapons, would you be more willing to risk it all in your pursuit of Finding Fabulous?

The Biggest Roadblock: You

Go as far as you can see; when you get there you'll be able to see farther.

J.P. Morgan

As I probed to understand the greatest challenges the FabFinders faced in their journeys, I discovered the most prominent one was "myself." I heard phrases like, "I just had to get out of my own way," or "I had to get over myself." Confessing the fear, anxiety, and self-doubt that crept into their thoughts, they revealed the factors that most often stalled their progress.

A budding entrepreneur confessed that, after decades of successive promotions at a top communications firm, she still struggled to understand her value outside of a corporate structure. One woman spoke of feeling like a fraud as she opened her own consulting business, despite having a master's degree and years of related experience. Another man told me he didn't think he "had what it takes" to build his own company, even though he had spent a decade advising some of the most prestigious companies in North America. Although their individual stories varied a great deal, there were common threads that wove their experiences together: a certain lack of self-confidence, a lack of knowledge about their value, and a feeling of not being credible enough. The more people I interviewed, the more I came to appreciate the prevalence and impact of self-limiting beliefs.

Maybe it is idealistic or naïve to think that anyone could go through a major transformation without self-doubt rearing its head. It certainly did in my case. Even though I was initially surprised to learn just how many FabFinders struggled with the same limiting beliefs I did, I was also quite reassured by it. If they could find ways around, over, or even through their issues, perhaps I could learn something from their examples. Maybe the solution to navigating my seemingly major roadblock was simpler than I thought.

Reviewing the many ways FabFinders "got in their own way," I started to see a pattern emerge, and I eventually came to understand how their most common issues fell into one or more of these five areas:

- **Awareness**—not knowing exactly what they wanted.

- **Value**—not understanding their value outside a formal, corporate structure.

- **Credibility**—thinking others wouldn't find them credible or qualified enough.

- **Confidence**—lacking self-confidence in their own ability.

- **Faith**—not believing it was possible or probable.

Digging deeper into how the FabFinders faced those issues, I found some lessons for overcoming some of my own self-limiting beliefs, along with ways to shorten my own learning curve. Although your story and situation are no doubt unique to you, I hope these examples give you some ideas and creative ways to tackle your own internal demons. Feel free to jump ahead to the one that resonates most with your story.

Awareness: Do you know what you want?

> *It is never too late*
> *to be what you might have been.*
>
> G. Eliot

"What do you want to be when you grow up?" is a question most often asked of small children. Whether the child wants to be a police officer, a banker, a ballerina, or a professional hockey player, the answers are often encouraged and even celebrated. I wanted to be a professional baseball player, until I wanted to be a teacher, and then a nurse, an Olympic gymnast, and eventually a doctor. I don't actually remember wanting to become all of those things, but luckily my mother kept a record of it in a special "School Days" memorabilia book. Recently I noticed something interesting as I flipped through the pages: the question, "What do you want to be when you grow up?" disappears. From grade seven to grade twelve, that section is replaced by one titled "honours and awards." It seems the focus shifts from what one wants to be to what one is good at. Why is that?

At what age should we stop considering who we want to *be* in lieu of the more "responsible" question of what we should *do* for a living? Although children's' answers often change as they grow and mature, it never ceases to amaze me how clear a five-year-old can be with the answer. Ask an adult the same question, and you'll get a completely different reaction.

Somewhere between kindergarten and adulthood, the natural awareness of what one wants gets lost. Disagree? Consider the multibillion-dollar industry that thrives on this very issue. Self-help books, courses, seminars, and other supporting products are being consumed at an ever-increasing rate. It seems millions of adults are still trying to figure out what they want to be when they grow up.

When was the last time you asked yourself that question? Consider me impressed, and equally envious, if you have a clear, concise answer; I've not been so lucky. When I asked one of the FabFinders why she became a lawyer in the first place, tears pooled in her eyes as she confessed she didn't know. Janel, our horse whisperer, recounted being swayed by her guidance counsellor to go into engineering when she was contemplating massage. Similarly, Tanya (the radio producer) recalls a nun at school telling her journalism wasn't an appropriate job for woman. It was rare for me to hear any of the FabFinders tell me they chose their initial profession purely for the joy of it.

So how does one go about figuring out what they want to be when they grow up?

Leo's Story

His smiling face and wagging tail let you know he's in heaven. He absolutely loves this! Playing fetch, swimming, or preferably both at the same time, is just in his blood. It is 100% what he was born (or more accurately, bred) to do. My yellow Labrador, Leo, teaches me many things, perhaps none more important than the joy that comes from being you.

Proudly prancing up a hill carrying a gigantic stick, or swiftly motoring through the water with a rubber toy locked between his jaws, it doesn't take long to see the impact his joy has on the world. People passing by point and laugh, and previously gruff-looking strangers break out into full-faced grins. They can't help themselves; his joy overflows and spills into their hearts. I've seen it many times; every time it brightens my day and reminds me of the power of being oneself.

Maybe it's easier for a dog, knowing exactly what makes them happy. Or perhaps self-doubt and lack of worthiness just aren't emotions that affect our furry friends. Nonetheless, the lesson is simple: follow the joy. Have the conviction to be yourself and the courage to do what makes you happy. Not only will it bring joy to you, the world will smile too!

As I consider the state of my own awareness over the last few decades, I realize how infrequently I contemplated what makes me happy. I mean really, really, "tail-waggingly" happy. In an effort to correct that mistake, I've recently invested a lot of time into understanding what I missed along the way.

How did I get so off course? How did I find myself in a state of not being able to answer the simple question, "What do you want to do?"

Figuring out What you Want

> *Your visions will become clear*
> *only when you look into your own heart.*
> *Who looks outside, dreams; who looks inside, awakes.*
>
> C.G. Jung

No matter which self-help book you read or which personal growth guru you listen to, it doesn't take long to learn that transformational change starts with awareness. It is the quintessential first step to getting what you want.

For some FabFinders, the awareness of what brought them joy came slowly over many years, while others intentionally dedicated weeks or months to the process. One high-level director told me years of voracious journaling finally revealed his passions. A pharmaceutical sales representative attended several personal growth seminars, investing hours each week to connecting what she values with what she does for a living. Others spoke of meditation and hypnosis as pathways to uncovering what they really wanted.

For me, I always had a sense that I would leave my company and do what I was meant to do when I figured it out. I don't know how or when I knew that, but my awareness at that time was on a fairly superficial level. I knew I wasn't overjoyed or energized by what I did for a living, but I didn't truly understand why. I had no idea what I really wanted, but as I already mentioned, I wasn't doing anything to figure it out. I went about my job, distracted by the busyness of the day-to-day tasks and the stress of deadlines. I was living my life by default instead of by design.

For so many years, I let my lack of awareness hold me back; it was the number one factor that limited my ability to move forward. So what do you do if that's you? Where do you start?

The Power of Noticing

It wasn't until I started to make a conscious decision to work on figuring it out that I gained the most clarity. One of the saddest moments of my entire career transformation was when my coach asked me, "What brings you joy?" My inability to answer that simple question brought me to tears. How could I possibly not know what brings me joy? How sad is that?

The first real breakthrough was hearing another life coach tell me to "notice what you are noticing." At first I thought this was a redundant, obvious statement. Don't we always notice what we are noticing? Otherwise, how do you term it "noticing" in the first place? Funny thing—once I put that statement into my consciousness, it worked! Anytime I felt really happy, energized, or "in the flow," I would pause and ask myself why. I'd do the same thing anytime I caught myself feeling bored, frustrated, or annoyed. I was able to capture my thoughts and feelings better simply by being more intentional about it.

Once I consciously shifted my attention from *what* I was feeling to *why* I was feeling it, I was able to figure out the answer to "What brings you joy?" As it turns out, this process also worked in reverse. Thinking of past experiences during different phases of my career, I started to see patterns emerge. I could remember when my job felt effortless, fun, and even invigorating, versus those times when I wanted to stick the proverbial pencil in my eye!

For example, I remember many Monday morning meetings when I was yawning an hour into them. Why was that? Why, after a restful weekend and a good night's sleep, was I tired after only sixty minutes? In retrospect, I remember those were the meetings where I felt the most useless and irrelevant. Either we had already discussed the issues several times over with no real solution, or the decision had already been made. The process drained my energy! However, if the direction of the meeting changed to include a creative solution-finding workshop, I would be bouncing out of my chair, fully engaged, without a yawn in sight. If I was asked to lead the session, I was even more awake and full of energy. Although this fairly simple exercise wasn't enough to provide all the answers I needed, it did provide some clues and taught me the power of increasing my own awareness.

Several of the FabFinders had to do similar work to heighten their awareness. Some of them did it intentionally, while others came by it more naturally. Hearing how they hired coaches to lead them through the process, learned new skills, or just dared to try new things, I learned that awareness comes from action. I found the real magic by listening to how the FabFinders leveraged that new awareness as a starting block.

Sometimes gaining new awareness can be painful. In Beena's case, it was quite literally painful, but as I quickly learned from her story, the end result can make it all worthwhile.

Beena's Story

Waking up in the ICU after a seemingly minor accident caused a life-threatening brain injury, Beena reached a critical turning point that changed her life forever. Although it was a scary, painful lesson, she's gained enough insight to be grateful for the awakening that resulted.

For many years prior to the accident, Beena had been working as an IT consultant for one of the top consulting firms in the US. Although she was well paid and enjoyed the variety of people she worked with, she was drained by the day-to-day grind of consulting. Believing that work wasn't supposed to be fun anyway, she kept plugging along. It wasn't until she took a hiatus to go to business school that her mindset started to shift. That daring decision to take a break from her career was the first real action she took to figuring out what she wanted. What she figured out was that work didn't have to be such a struggle—if she could only find work to which she was better suited.

With her genuine interest in consumer behaviour, she seemed to be a perfect fit for brand management, so it was there that Beena made her next pit stop on her path to Finding Fabulous. That role suited her better than her job as an IT consultant, but it still left her feeling that something was missing. This time, however, it took a major wake-up call before she did anything about it.

It wasn't until that fateful day in the ICU that her eyes were truly opened. The realization that her injuries could have been much worse led to a sense of deep gratitude, along with many questions. What was her legacy to this world? Did she even matter? If God spared her life, was she meant to do something bigger? Not knowing what that "something bigger" might be, Beena signed up for a coaching course so she could work herself through it. Admittedly sceptical about the entire process of coaching, she attempted to hide in the back of the room and simply watch, but fate proved to have a different plan: the teacher walked right up and selected her for the first activity.

Beena's voice boomed across Skype as she recalled the moment. "It was probably the best thing that could have happened, because in that session the coach unlocked something that was deep within me. It gave me this light. I came back from that coaching event and I was on fire!" she exclaimed. "I had never gotten this excited about anything before. Something just awakened inside of me. It was a light bulb moment. I wanted to start a revolution of women around the globe—women who were playing small, settling for mediocre lives. Helping these women ignite their 'personal revolutions' would be my legacy, and it would change the world!"

That first coaching session helped Beena clarify her mission and her passion. Suddenly conscious of how much she had been hiding her true self at work, she resolved to help others understand and uncover their own worth. She believes that being who you truly are leads to even greater success, and she knows the first step is doing the work to figure it out.

Being aware of what one wants doesn't mean having all of the answers; it requires intentionally living, striving to uncover the answers on a consistent basis. Beena didn't know that she would go from IT to marketing and eventually to coaching. Leaving that first job to pursue an MBA was a key step toward finding more joy in her work. It was the first commitment she made in her journey to finding more fabulous.

Many of the other FabFinders spoke about this idea of following the breadcrumbs to their ideal lives. Often, they would become aware of something they wanted to do, only to discover later that it was just a stepping stone toward what they were really passionate about. The important thing is that they needed to take the first step in order to become aware of the second—or third, or fourth!

This was the biggest difference I found between the FabFinders and those I spoke to who were suffering and miserable. So many people talked about feeling trapped by their jobs or frustrated by their work. When I asked what they were doing about it, I often got a shoulder shrug or a resigned, "I don't know what else to do." The FabFinders, on the other hand, made the conscious decision to figure it out. Shifting their mindset from suffering to inquiry was empowering because it instigated the actions that moved them forward. Those small actions had huge impacts, transforming their fears about being stuck and bringing them to the realization that their situations were just temporary. Whether they took workshops to uncover their passions, read books, watched videos, signed up for courses, or just re-evaluated what they liked about their current jobs, they were taking steps in the right direction.

What are you doing to uncover what brings you joy? Do you know who you want to be when you grow up? If not, what are you doing to increase your awareness? What small action could you take today to shift your attention from what you *don't* want to what you *do* want?

Value: What do you have to offer?

*Too many people overvalue what they are not
and undervalue what they are.*

Malcolm S. Forbes

Sitting cross-legged on the floating dock as I soaked up the morning sun and absorbed the sounds and smells of the freshwater lake, I had a little epiphany. A little birdy came and whispered it in my ear. Okay, that's not exactly true, but it felt like that.

At the time, I was trying to figure out what I was going to do for a living. Despite investing money in life coaches and hours in online personal growth courses, I was struggling. Even though I had a greater awareness of what I wanted, I still wasn't completely clear about my value. Everywhere I looked, it seemed like someone was already doing what I wanted to do. I didn't know what else I had to offer. Sure, I had skills—fifteen years of corporate sales, marketing, and people management taught me a thing or two, but how was that different from anyone else? How was I unique?

As a marketer, I was quite familiar with the importance of having a unique value proposition. I knew that every good business plan starts there. I knew I would have to be clear about mine if I was going to be successful at opening my own business. But how the heck do you do that? How do you find the *unique* in what you do, when it seems like everyone else is already doing it and every new idea you have has already been thought of?

As I sat in stillness on the dock that day, I started to appreciate how innately unique each of us are. As I listened to the cacophony of chirps, trills, whirls, and squawks echo across the lake, it occurred to me: every single bird added to the experience. No bird was the same; even birds of the same species had their own rhythms, tones, and volume. That morning was so memorable and profound because of the simple, sheer beauty of this orchestra-like performance. There was not one sound that I wished would fade away.

What do you think would happen if any of those birds had an identity crisis like mine, and decided not to sing? What if, just when they were about to open their beaks, they heard other birds and thought, "I guess they don't need my voice"? What if they decided they had nothing else to offer?

That's when it occurred to me: maybe we aren't that different from those symphonic birds. Each and every one of us has a unique voice that adds value to the whole. No other person has the same combination of growing up the way we did, experiencing the things we have, or seeing the world the way we do. We don't have to create our value or invent our uniqueness; we're born with it!

Understanding and Accepting Your Value

One of the benefits of working for a structured company is that they give you a title and an associated salary. Most of them list the skills and abilities that go along with the title, clearly outlining the role you'll play in the overall organization. If you work in teams, often roles are defined and allocated based on others' perceptions of what you can offer. In essence, *they* tell *you* your value. The FabFinders spoke of the challenge this posed when they left those formalized frameworks behind. Outside of those corporate walls, what was their value? What did they have to offer, and how valuable was that to other people?

The degree of this challenge varied for FabFinders, depending on whether they were struggling to find their purpose, establishing themselves in a new industry, or simply trying to brand a new business. What value does a people manager offer if she isn't managing people? To what degree can a previous administrative assistant help someone looking for a personal trainer? What strength does a structural engineer provide to owners of distressed horses?

Similar to heightening awareness around what brings you joy, understanding and accepting the value you offer can take some work. Fortunately, the FabFinders' experiences provide some clues about how we can start to uncover the value we offer the world.

Value in Feedback

There's a reason for the expression, "… can't see the forest for the trees." After all, it's hard to see the bigger picture when you're too close to it. I believe this can be the case with perceiving our own value. Sometimes the things we do best are the very things we take most for granted. These are the skills and talents we don't even consider strengths because they feel too easy. Have you ever had someone tell you how great you are at something, only to think, "Oh that—it's nothing"? Maybe it's time to ask those people to remind you what those things are.

Susan's Story

> *After leaving a multinational communications company without knowing what she would do, Susan struggled to understand her value. Despite a successful career that had spanned nearly thirty years, she wasn't sure what she could offer as an entrepreneur.*

Marketing courses taught her the importance of differentiating herself and preached the practice of formulating her value into an offering for the people she wished to serve, but how could she do that when she wasn't even sure what value she offered?

With her severance package running out soon, Susan knew she couldn't afford to let the issue stall her progress any longer. She was confident enough in her performance at her previous position, so she decided to leverage the relationships she had developed over the years by reaching out to previous clients and colleagues for feedback. Their collective responses taught her how much people valued her leadership style and skills—things she had taken for granted. That insight gave her permission to start her own leadership consulting and coaching business; it was the first clue to designing her perfect job. Whether or not this ends up being her version of fabulous, it has given Susan the first stepping stone to her future.

Are you clear about the value you offer the world? What do people say they appreciate most about you? Who could you ask for feedback? How might insight into what makes you unique help you move forward?

Value in Changing Perspective

A side effect of working in any one position, with any one company, and/or within one particular industry for long enough is that you start to have a bit of tunnel vision. This affects our perception of possibilities and distorts our understanding of the value of certain experiences. Assets, skills, and talents required for certain roles can start to seem so basic that we forget the true value in them. For example, if you are constantly asked to present in front of groups of people, whether or not your job officially requires it, you can end up "accidentally" becoming an amazing speaker. A sales representative who is required to build strategic business plans each quarter might end up with stronger strategizing skills than selling abilities.

Understanding my own value is an issue I still struggle with today, often under-rating the skills I've picked up along the way. I can't tell you how many times people have suggested that I become a coach. Whether it's because I provided an ear to a girlfriend who's just ended a relationship, brainstormed with a colleague about a new business venture, or helped a family member tackle career challenges, the suggestion has come up many times.

My initial reaction is the same every time: I'm not a coach. I don't have any training or certifications. But the more I work to uncover what I enjoyed about my previous jobs, the more I realize that's not entirely true. For years I managed sales representatives. One of my main roles involved developing the reps' selling skills, time management proficiency, data analysis abilities, business strategies, and communication effectiveness. Essentially, I was every bit as much a coach as I was a manager, just without the formal title. The only thing that stopped me from being a coach in another environment, or within another industry, was my own perception of my abilities.

What strengths and talents do you take for granted? Could widening your perspective and changing your frame of reference open up new possibilities for your future?

Value in Irritation

Innovation is a word that's tossed around loosely these days, as if it's a title or honour to strive for. "Be innovative" is something I often heard in my corporate days, and just as often it irritated the crap out of me! People aren't innovative because someone tells them to be. People are innovative because they are irritated, frustrated, or annoyed enough to be motivated to find a better solution. The better you are at coming up with creative new solutions, the more likely you are to find your innovation.

This is something else I learned from the FabFinders—the value of being irritated. The irritated hockey mom turns in her gavel and leaves her job as a district judge to coach, empower, and inspire greatness in young athletes. The irritated business owner decides to tee up her ability to translate golf skills to the boardroom by empowering businessmen. Angela was an irritated sales rep who decided to turn the stethoscope on the doctors, challenging their ability to be role models for health.

Angela's Story

Angela had no idea the thing that irritated her most would end up being the driving force behind her true purpose. After seventeen years working with family physicians, she started to feel disconnected with her role as a sales representative. It took several personal growth seminars, along with many additional hours working on herself, before she started to understand what she valued most in life.

She enjoyed the close relationships she had developed with physicians, but it bothered her that they were the unhealthiest people she knew. How could these physicians be role models for their patients when they didn't practice what they preached? Initially, her dissatisfaction, coupled with the sense she wasn't making a difference, led her to leave pharmaceuticals to train as a corporate coach. Although she enjoyed the coaching part, she struggled to connect with the environment of large corporations, and she continued to long for more meaning in her work.

It wasn't until she connected her highest values with what irritated her most that she found what she was looking for. She realized that she could have a greater impact on a larger number of people if she trained physicians to be better role models for healthy living, and they in turn passed this knowledge on to their patients. As an energy and life coach, Angela teaches doctors the roles of nutrition, exercise, and mindfulness in overall health. Stressing the importance of self-care, she reminds physicians to start practicing what they preach. Who knew the very reason Angela left her job would end up becoming her greatest mission?

Have you ever found yourself in a situation like Angela's, when you became irritated or frustrated that no one had come up with a solution to some obvious problem? Did you ever stop to think you might be so irritated because *you* are the one meant to find the solution? How can you take something that irritates you and turn it into a mission that gives your life new meaning and provides your career with a much-needed reboot?

Credibility: What will everyone think?

> *You wouldn't worry so much about what others think of you
> if you realized how seldom they do.*
>
> Eleanor Roosevelt

What makes an expert an expert? How much experience is enough? What level of education would suffice? Am I qualified? Am I good enough? Am I worthy enough?

I wondered, as I did research for this book, how many interviews I would have to do before it was enough. At first the question was related completely to my desire to uncover truth and relevance for my readers. I knew my own story would not provide a complete picture, so I endeavoured to find enough variety in the stories of others. I have to admit that my own self-limiting beliefs started to creep in as I wondered how many interviews other people would say were enough for me to have a pertinent opinion on the topic. Some people might think fifty interviews were enough; others might say a hundred, or even a thousand. In the end, I determined "enough" was based on the information I garnered from the FabFinders and how often I came across repeated patterns. In essence, at some point I had to trust my gut and let go of the rest.

The clearer I became on what I wanted and how I thought I could best serve others, the more trustworthy my gut instincts became. In the case of this book, I genuinely want to help people find more fabulous in their lives. I want the examples of others to provide inspiration, challenge the status quo, and redefine perceptions of what's possible. There is no perfect number of interviews that will accomplish these goals. I'm not promising results or claiming to have all the answers; I'm simply hypothesizing what could be possible and daring readers to do the same. Did I do enough? You get to decide that for yourself while I work on accepting and believing in my own credibility to have a "good enough" opinion on the matter.

Many of the FabFinders told me they didn't feel qualified to do what they were doing, and they worried about whether people would believe they were credible. Apparently I wasn't the only one with this issue. Some even admitted to feeling like a fraud or recounted that reaching the success they longed for didn't change the fact that they never felt good enough. Most relevant for the rest of us, they didn't let their doubts keep them from *Finding Fabulous*— they did it anyway! In some cases it might have delayed their actions or challenged their choices, but they were brave enough to push forward in spite of themselves.

So where did they build up that courage? How does one do that?

Recently I was listening to Scott Dinsmore (of *Live Your Legend*) describe a practical way to move past issues of credibility: focus on helping just one person before you worry about how to help hundreds or thousands. Scott reminds people that all experts started somewhere and built up their expertise as they went along.

Leaving a job he hated to find work that matters, Scott built a successful business around helping others do the same. He has created an online community of people trying to do work that matters, and he offers tons of free advice and tools to help people uncover their passions. He also sells courses that teach them how to make a living doing it.

In Scott's case, the more he helped individuals, one-on-one, decide if they should leave their jobs, the more people asked for his help. He soon began to recognize patterns in the types of issues and questions they had, and he was able to scale his advice to a bigger audience. In essence, his credibility came from doing something instead of waiting to do something until he had the credibility.

Remember Shelagh, the teacher who wanted to spend more time with her children? Her story is a great example of how a strong motivation for change can trump the fear of not feeling credible enough.

Shelagh's Story, continued:

> *As you might remember, Shelagh was a public school teacher before she left it all behind to start her own training and consulting business. She recalls that, despite having a master's degree in curriculum development and learning, she felt like a fraud in the early years*

when she was creating her business and her brand. Even though she had worked for another corporate training company, she didn't have experience at a Fortune 500 firm or the credentials of an MBA. The absence of those three letters on her business card left her wondering if people would believe she had something to offer. Combine that with the fact that most of her relatives had the higher education and experience she was lacking, and her self-confidence rested on shaky ground.

In order to overcome her fears and move her business forward, Shelagh leveraged her desire for change. The importance of having more freedom with her time in order to raise her small children trumped her fear of whether others might think she was qualified enough. It was just enough to help her get started. The more entrepreneurs she worked with, the more credibility she gained from the results they achieved.

Fortunately for Shelagh and the thousands of business owners who benefit from her teaching, she didn't let her fears paralyze her and keep her from moving forward toward her version of fabulous. The success of her business is evidence that credibility can be achieved along the way.

Are you worried that others might not find you credible enough to do the work you want to do? If so, how can you start to build that credibility? Remember Scott Dinsmore's advice and Shelagh's example: think of some small way to help even one person, and then another, and another. What could you accomplish if you spent more time building your credibility and less time worrying about it?

Confidence: Are you capable?

> *Always remember you are braver than you believe, stronger than you seem and smarter than you think.*
>
> **Christopher Robin**

It's a *Duck Dynasty* world! That's what I like to say to people who lack the self-confidence to do the things they're passionate about, or who wonder if there's any chance that they can make a living doing it. If you aren't familiar with the colourful cast of characters from this popular TV reality show, I'm talking about the Robertson family from *Duck Dynasty*. They're a lively group of individuals from West Monroe, Louisiana who, along with captivating millions of viewers each week, make a lot of money selling duck calls and related duck-hunting paraphernalia.

The reason this family caught my attention in the first place was the unique nature of their business. It's not every day that you read about someone becoming a millionaire because of a love of duck hunting. It fascinates me that someone (the patriarch of the family, Phil Robertson) represents the very ideal I've come to respect and appreciate. No, I'm not talking about long beards and redneck living! I'm talking about the idea of following your passion and creating your own fabulous life. This is a story about a man who turned down the opportunity to play professional football because it interfered with duck hunting season. He had a very clear passion, and decided his life was going to include, and even revolve around, that passion, so he made it happen.

I don't know if he intended or expected his decision to eventually make him a millionaire, but his is a great example of how someone can make a life by living his or her passion—he literally, and figuratively, found his "calling."

In searching for my own "duck dynasty," I've met some great people who are doing just that. I've also met a lot of people who would rather be doing something else, but they've convinced themselves they can't. To them I say, "It's a *Duck Dynasty* world." Find your duck. What are you passionate about? If you know, then go do it! With so many resources available in today's globally connected, digital world, the chance that you can actually make a living at whatever you are passionate about is more possible (and even probable) than ever before. We'll talk about how to find your passion later in this chapter. Right now, the important thing is to focus on discovering if you have the confidence to pursue it.

FabFinders were not immune to issues of self-confidence, but they were able to teach me some new and different ways to get past them. Remember Jess, the law clerk who wanted to find the money to get married? She found a company with extensive training and strong support, which was the key to overcoming her shyness and gaining enough self-confidence to thrive in the network marketing industry. Susan, the former communications executive, was able to leverage her reputation and past experience in the corporate world to gain the confidence she needed to start her own company.

Given the success of his adventure travel company, it's hard to imagine a time when my friend Chris didn't have the self-confidence to start his own business. It wasn't until the concept of entrepreneurism was "demystified" that his mindset started to shift.

Chris' Story

Chris didn't initially have aspirations to start his own company. "I had built it up in my mind to be something unattainable for me, and thought I didn't have the risk tolerance. I just thought I wasn't cut out for that," he explains. Throughout his career at one of the top management consulting firms in the US, Chris had mostly worked with large, well-established companies, and never had the experience of being inside an entrepreneurial environment or a start-up.

Despite the fact that his firm was preparing him for future partnership, Chris knew he didn't want to work in a large corporate environment any more. "I wasn't passionate enough about the work I was doing or motivated by the rewards to compensate for it," he says.

After accepting a severance package from his firm, Chris had the opportunity to spend some time reflecting and assessing his options. "I wanted to work with a small enough company that I could really make an impact that I could see and feel, one I could really get my arms around." By then, he had come to realize that he could have much more fun consulting for companies if he was excited about the product or service.

One such experience happened when he spent a year consulting with an adventure travel company. The contacts he retained from that job made it fairly easy to explore new opportunities in that industry, and it didn't take Chris long to find a start-up company that fit his criteria. Although that opportunity was ultimately short-lived, the insights he gained from his involvement provided him with a couple of "light-bulb" moments. "It demystified a lot of things for me," he says, "I found out being an entrepreneur wasn't rocket science. It's a ton of work, and there are a lot of challenges and stresses, but these guys are just kind of figuring it out as they go along."

Immediately following his departure from that firm, he went to work on a new business model for his own startup idea. Still hesitant about his ability to start his own business, Chris interviewed with some private equity firms as a fallback measure, but he felt less and less connected with the idea of going back, and he wondered if he was selling himself short. With strong support from his friends and an extra push from his wife, he realized, "I have to do this. I'm going to regret it if I don't give it a shot."

Reflecting on the first couple of years as the owner of his company, Chris is able to appreciate the success that supports his family financially while enabling him and his wife to travel. "To have taken something that didn't exist and make it a reality, and to have driven it all, is very gratifying." Although he admits that there are always new challenges, and it can be easy to get distracted, overall he knows that he has built a strong foundation. Chris sums it up by offering these words of wisdom: "You always ask yourself if you are investing in the right areas and doing everything you can reasonably do. Then, at some point you just have to let go and have the confidence the results will come."

After speaking to many entrepreneurs, FabFinders, and others struggling to find the confidence to follow their dreams, I have come to believe that lack of confidence comes from our imagination. I think we build up the idea that something is impossible by *imagining* what it would take instead of *figuring out* what it would take. Chris's perception of what it took to own his own company was only demystified after he had some experience working with people who were doing just that. Seeing "behind the curtain" of that operation showed him that he didn't need to have all the answers. He learned that he could figure it out along the way. In the same way, Jess believed she was too shy to make presentations in front of a group until she actually started to do it.

Once again, it seems the FabFinders show us that action is the key. Are you being held back by the belief that something is too hard or out of your reach? Where could you go to find other people doing those "impossible" things? What is one thing you could learn or experience to prove to yourself just how capable you are?

Faith: Do you believe it's possible?

> *You must expect great things of yourself before you can do them.*
>
> Michael Jordan

Have you heard the story about the man who kept praying he would win the lottery? He walks into church week after week, praying that God will help him win the lottery so he can take care of his family. Eventually angry with God for not answering his prayers, he shouts his confusion at the sky, demanding to know why. As the story goes, God's voice booms down: "For Heaven's sake, buy a ticket!"

Whether you believe in God or not isn't really the point I wanted to make here. It's more about the story's lesson about faith in general and what we do with it. First of all, the man in the story supposedly believes in God and his ability to help him win the lottery. If he indeed believes that God answers prayers, why does he continue to go back week after week? What kind of faith is that? Wouldn't it be logical to assume that God heard him the first time? After asking for what he needs, the man presumably makes no effort to set himself up to receive what he asked for; otherwise, he'd have bought a ticket. What does that say about his overall faith that he can have what he wants?

If I were to identify one common theme running through all the self-help books I've read, courses I've completed, experts I've listened to, and coaches I've worked with, it would be the importance of faith. Faith in one's self, faith in one's abilities, and faith in the idea that anything is possible: these seem to be the catalysts for getting what you want. The Law of Attraction states that, after gaining clarity about what you want, you have to believe it is possible, then act like you already have it. Now that's faith!

After listening and re-listening to the recordings of all the interviews I conducted with the FabFinders, I started to sense an often unspoken, and perhaps under-realized, key to success. Even though they gave me some great answers to the question about success and offered some practical advice for others, there seemed to be something they weren't saying. Those who were most successful (as determined by their own definitions and recognition that they had achieved, and were living, their versions of fabulous) seemed to possess a strong, almost indefinable, unshakeable faith that everything would work out. Perhaps no single person's story illustrates this concept more clearly than Michael's.

Michael's Story

> *What kind of faith is necessary to go on stage in front of hundreds of people and perform a hypnosis act, when you've never hypnotized anyone in your entire life? That's a question you'd have to ask Michael.*
>
> *Having left a stable, relatively lucrative auto factory job to try his hand at entrepreneurship, Michael found himself stuck, making less money and working more hours. Unfortunately, he had invested all of his money in buying a cookie store franchise that was struggling in post-recession times. Not that passionate about the business of selling cookies, Michael spent most of his time doing magic tricks for his customers.*

One day, a customer suggested that Michael's magic show would be a great way to entertain guests waiting for tables at restaurants. Jumping at the opportunity, it was long before Michael found himself earning more from his magic act than his cookie business. Around the same time, Michael went to see an entertaining hypnotist named Mike Mandel. Enjoyment quickly turned to fascination, as Michael realized he wanted to become a hypnotist.

*His desire was so strong that when he was offered the opportunity to perform his magic at a local college, he told them he was a hypnotist. Convincing them to book him for hypnosis instead of his usual magic show meant that he had only three months to figure out how to actually **be** a hypnotist. He started recording every hypnosis act he could find, dissecting the tapes to build what he calls a "giant matrix of hypnosis shows." Exemplifying the true magic of faith, he chose to perform in front of 250 people, despite having never hypnotized anyone in his life. He was nearly as surprised as his audience (or perhaps even more so) when it actually worked!*

Despite the impressive chutzpa that must have taken, he admits his thoughts weren't always as courageous as his actions would imply. He admits, "I used to sit at home thinking, 'Who do you think you are? You can't do this! Quit dreaming and go back to work!'" Luckily, he didn't.

To this day, the result of that experience still fuels Michael's faith in what is possible if you want it badly enough. "I will never be as scared spit-less as I was that day, on that stage, when I didn't know if I could do it. Nothing will ever be harder than that," he says with conviction. "I figure if I can do that, I can do anything!"

This idea of faith is one that I think is often underrated and underappreciated. There is only so much you can do to increase your skills, your confidence, your awareness, and your sense of worthiness or value. At some point in the journey, you have to let go and have a little faith that it will all work out. Michael was clear that he wanted to be a hypnotist, and he was confident enough that he could teach himself how to do it, but in the end it took an admirable level of faith for him to stand up on that stage and believe it would all work out. Chris's story is very similar: even after he gained the confidence to open his own business, he still admits he had to let go and have faith the results would come.

As I've gone through my own journey of Finding Fabulous, my faith has been tested many times. I believed in going after my dreams, but was I being as brave as Michael was when he walked onto that stage? I'm confident in my abilities to be an entrepreneur, so why was I so hesitant to start? Did I have enough faith that the results would come?

The casual conversations I've had with friends, acquaintances, and sometimes even strangers over the past couple of years have revealed an interesting dichotomy. Some people, regardless of their awareness of what they want or their confidence in their skill sets, don't really believe it's possible. Instead they speak about the world being unfair, or how easy it is for other people who don't share their circumstances. No matter how many stories I recount of others who've overcome similar situations, their belief (or disbelief) is unshakeable.

What about you? Is a lack of faith holding you back or making you anxious? Do you have faith that you can have everything you want? What are you doing to demonstrate or strengthen that faith?

Roadmap: Get Out of Your Own Way

> *The fastest way to do the things you think can't be done is to surround yourself with people already doing them.*
>
> **Scott Dinsmore**

Now it's your turn. Are you getting in your own way? Which self-limiting beliefs are holding you back or slowing your progress?

- **Awareness**—not knowing exactly what you want
- **Value**—not understanding your value outside a formal corporate structure
- **Credibility**—thinking others won't find you credible or qualified enough
- **Confidence**—lacking self-confidence in your own ability
- **Faith**—not believing it's possible or probable

Awareness

Do you know what you want?

Both Beena and I had to do some work to figure out what we wanted to do. I focused on asking myself some basic questions about what brought me joy and what drained my energy. Intentionally shifting my attention taught me about the power of noticing and gave me clues to move forward. Beena's path included going back to school to learn new skills, working in a new industry, and taking on a new role, in addition to seeking coaching as a means to understand her passions. Each step provided her with more of the information she needed to find her version of fabulous.

- ☐ Do you know what you want to do?

If so, what is holding you back?

If not, try one of these techniques:

- ✓ Notice what brings you joy or drains your energy.
- ✓ Try new things, travel to new places, go out and meet new people, and stay aware of things that bring you joy and new possibilities you may not have considered.
- ✓ Hire a coach or find a mentor to help you.
- ✓ Start a journal and write down how you feel when you are doing various activities and tap into what you really want.

Value

Do you understand what unique value you have to offer?

Susan was able to uncover her value for serving others by asking those whom she had served. Despite working for herself in a completely new environment, she understood that the value she offered was transferrable and something she could be confident about. Angela realized that the very thing that irritated her most about her job could be her new mission. Providing a solution instead of fighting the frustration, she has become valuable in a completely unexpected way. In my story, I had to look at my coaching experience from a new perspective to see the value I could offer.

☐ Do you understand your value or unique offering?

If so, what is holding you back from delivering it to the world?

If not, try one of these techniques:

- ✓ Ask friends, co-workers and family members what they think you do better than anyone else.
- ✓ Think about things or situations that irritate you, and consider whether you want to help find a solution.
- ✓ Take Strength Finder 2.0 or other validated tests to uncover your strengths and value.

- ✓ Make a list of skills and talents you have used in other jobs or roles and consider how translatable those skills are to other positions (don't forget to include volunteer experiences, athletics, and even roles you play with friends and family).

Credibility

Do you worry whether people will think you are qualified enough?

Shelagh struggled with feeling like a fraud because she assumed people would want her to have specific degrees or experience in a Fortune 500 company. Focusing on the reasons she wanted her own business in the first place gave her enough confidence to get started. The more individuals she was able to help, the less those degrees seemed to matter. At some point she just had to push through her own insecurities and do it anyway. It is in the doing where the credibility builds, and with results the fear of what's lacking fades away.

- ☐ Do you struggle with feeling credible? Do you stress about whether other people will think you are qualified enough to do what you want to do?

If not, then what is holding you back from doing what you want to do? If so, try one of these techniques:

- ✓ Build up your confidence in your credibility little by little (e.g., concentrate on helping just one person, then build from there).
- ✓ List all the reasons you think people won't find you credible, then come up with a reason or counterpoint to each of them that explains why you *are* credible (this forces you to remember all the skills and experience you may be forgetting you have).

Confidence

Do you have confidence in your ability to do what you want to do?

When Chris first considered being an entrepreneur, he didn't think he had what it takes. His own misperceptions of possible were only challenged when he allowed himself the opportunity to see other entrepreneurs in action.

Demystifying what it takes to start a business, Chris proved Scott Dinsmore's quote correct: "the fastest way to do the things you think can't be done, is to hang around people already doing them."

☐ Does a lack of self-confidence hold you back?

If not, then what does?

If so, try one of these techniques:

- ✓ Learn from someone doing what you want to do.
- ✓ Find a mentor to help get you started.
- ✓ Take a calculated risk and try it anyway!

Faith

Do you believe you can have what you want?

Michael demonstrated what it means to "act as if" when he put himself on that stage in front of all those people without knowing for sure that he could do it. It was a huge leap of faith! You don't have to be as brave as Michael, but consider whether you generally have faith that things will turn out.

☐ Do you have faith that what you want is possible?

If so, then what else could be holding you back?

If not, try some of these techniques:

- ✓ Listen to inspirational speakers who speak to your beliefs and challenge you to dream big.
- ✓ Research stories of others who have accomplished great things in the face of major challenges.
- ✓ Spend time with others who are accomplishing great things that you find admirable.
- ✓ Spend time with others who tell you it can be done and encourage your progress.

Chapter 4: Money

*What is a cynic?
A man who knows the price of everything
and the value of nothing.*

Oscar Wilde

Have you ever seen a million dollars in cash? I mean seen it in real life, not on a TV show or in a movie. I'll never forget the first time I held that much money in my hands—or, more accurately, hefted in my arms. It was during my summer break from university, while I was working at the main office of a major Canadian bank. The first time I created a million-dollar package, I was struck by the sheer size and weight of it. It definitely challenged my Hollywood-inspired belief that several million bucks could fit into a small briefcase. Even more surprising than the actual size of the parcel was how much the experience of handling it impacted my perception of its value.

The cash room was where the really big parcels were prepared. I remember the first time I was locked into that vault-like room in the cold basement of the bank. I knew that I'd be surrounded by millions of dollars, more money than I had ever seen. All day we would count money that came in from local businesses, including the larger deposits from the US–Canada Bridge and Tunnel accounts. We'd verify the deposits, bundle the bills, and prepare parcels for the Brinks truck that would carry the funds away again. That first day, as I was leaving the vault to take lunch, I glanced down at my hands, shocked to see how black they were. Grossed out by the gritty black filth, I headed straight to the bathroom to scrub them clean. As I scrubbed harder, digging at the dirt beneath my nails, I had a bit of an ah-ha moment: money is just dirty paper! No matter how much we try to romanticize what it means to have a lot of it, or fault our misfortunes for the lack of it, money is literally just dirty paper.

Since that day's revelation, I can honestly say that I believe the value of money rests in the hands of the holder. That summer, for me, money meant tasks that had to be done: bills that needed sorting, stacking, and wrapping. It required standing for hours on end, avoiding paper cuts, and lifting heavy parcels. It was an education in the value of money, literally and figuratively. It meant if I could earn enough of the "dirty stuff," I could pay for another year's tuition. It was a means to an end, not the end itself. Money is never the end goal; it's merely a means of getting other things you want. Since that summer, I've used the memory of my grimy hands, along with the phrase "it's just dirty paper," to keep the value of money in perspective.

So how do we do that?

As we discussed in chapter 3, understanding what you want and why is a critical starting point. After all, how can you know how much money you need to make your dreams come true if you don't know what your dreams are? How can you calculate what you are willing to do for those dreams, if you don't appreciate why you want to change? The FabFinders started there. It wasn't until they felt a strong enough longing for more purpose or a deep desire for more freedom that they had adequate incentive to figure out the money part. A driving motivation for change was the catalyst that drove them to re-evaluate their perspective on the need for money, along with its value and limitations.

What about you? Are you letting money hold you back? In this journey of finding a better life, what role does money play?

Think of it another way:

> If I could write you a check right now for the exact amount of money (no more, no less) it would take to give you the courage to drop everything and go after your dreams, how much would that be? What would you do if money were no object?

What is money worth to you?

In the course of discovering how the FabFinders valued money, I uncovered both interesting similarities and surprising differences. Various factors influenced their thoughts, affected their beliefs, and, in turn, impacted their actions. It didn't take too many interviews to conclude that a book about *Finding Fabulous* would need an entire chapter devoted to money. After all, there isn't much we can do without at least a certain amount of the green stuff. Even so, it still fascinated me to learn how frequently people use it as a crutch and how often it distracts from other issues. Money seems to be the number one, big fat hairy elephant in the room.

"I'd love to do that, but I have bills to pay." I heard this statement, in one form or another, over and over again whenever I described the focus of the book and the courageous stories of the FabFinders to other people. Surprisingly, the comment wasn't unique to people who struggled with money; it was voiced by people from all walks of life. Some were afraid they wouldn't be able to pay the rent, while others worried they wouldn't be able to send their kids to exclusive summer camps, but the objection or obstacle seemed the same.

As we learned from Abraham Maslow in the 1940s, people's motivation to meet different needs moves through a hierarchy. It stands to reason that an individual who is struggling to feed or shelter himself will have a different perspective on *Finding Fabulous* then someone who has large sums of disposable income. The basic need to put food on the table will undoubtedly trump the need to make a positive impact on the world. That being said, FabFinders' examples provide a new perspective on the role of money and offer ways to keep it from blocking our progress throughout this journey.

A former teacher learned the more she worried about money, the tougher it seemed to get. Initially struggling to find the right students for her tutoring business, she had to learn to shift her focus to the value she offered. Becoming more valuable to the students she already had seemed to "magically" draw new students to her. A speaking coach learned how to leverage the necessity of taking on side jobs in order to support his family of five. Instead of accepting any job that would pay him, he learned to intentionally choose opportunities that put him in close proximity with potential customers. An IT consultant-turned-photographer chose to supplement her income with real estate investments. This removed the pressure she felt to build a bigger nest egg for retirement, and the added income meant she didn't have to compromise the quality of her work by extending her hours or changing her prices.

Depending on the path each of the FabFinders took, the issues surrounding money ranged from being nonexistent to posing a major roadblock. For those for whom money was an issue, it was not always the toughest to overcome. One could argue that the issues related to "you" (explained in the previous chapter) are more difficult to unravel than solutions for money issues that are more tangible and simpler to plan for. After all, the need for $10,000 is a lot more tangible than the need to believe you're worthy of great success. How do you measure worthiness? Although I am not attempting to quantify any one challenge in relation to another (I leave that up to you), I will present some concepts I learned along the way that illustrate this point.

The concepts and suggestions presented in this chapter are meant to help you expose your beliefs about money and challenge whether it is the primary issue that prevents you from *Finding Fabulous*. Arguably more important than any dollar amount I could write on that "dream" check, the FabFinders taught me the value of understanding these three things:

- **Key Influencers**—What affects our thoughts about the value of money?

- **Need vs. Want**—Where do we draw the line between need and want?

- **Willingness**—What impacts our willingness to do what it takes?

Regardless of the degree to which money played a role, each interview offered some interesting insights that might help others daring to follow a similar path. Even though the examples don't solve every possible money problem, I believe they offer creative solutions for generating, supplementing, and/or replacing income sources while redefining how much money you need to get started. The following stories are intended to encourage you to think differently about money and dare you to consider what opportunities you might miss if you don't.

Key Influencers

What affects our thoughts about money?

The amount of money your parents had while you were growing up—whether they relied on a steady paycheck working the line at Ford or balanced the uncertainty of an entrepreneurial income—will undoubtedly give you a unique perspective. If you lived in a mansion and attended the best boarding schools, your definitions of rich and poor will differ greatly from someone who survived on food stamps and public education. Those who grew up always competing to have what everyone else had, as opposed to people raised with a sense of gratitude and service, will have different views on the connection between money and fulfillment. Possibilities for the future may look completely different for a young, single adult than for a married couple with a child, or even a single father of four.

The intention of this book is not to debate how much money someone needs to *Find Fabulous*, nor to determine the amount on that fictitious check that will make you feel successful. Everyone has a right to his or her own opinion. However, after researching this topic for the past few years, I firmly believe there is value in spending the time and energy necessary to gain a better perspective about your own opinions. Identifying how and why you formed your opinions in the first place may help you determine if your thoughts about money are holding you back.

The variety of situations I found in the interviews led me to understand three main areas of influence that affected how the FabFinders positioned money in relation to other challenges:

      Personal Experience—"That's just how I grew up."

2.   **Comparative Analysis**—"Keeping up with the Joneses"

3.   **Debts & Obligations**—"I have a family to feed."

While you read the FabFinders' stories, consider which of these things has the biggest influence on your perception of money. Are any of these influencers affecting your decision to go out and find your version of fabulous?

Personal Experience

> *Empty pockets never held anyone back.*
> *Only empty heads and empty hearts can do that.*
>
> **Norman Vincent Peale**

Just prior to leaving my corporate job, I was having dinner with a close friend when she said, "We don't live in a world where Lisa Dadd goes hungry." And I believed her. Why? Was I being naïve about the realities, or arrogant about my abilities? How could I be so certain, when I had absolutely no idea what I was going to do for a living?

At a very young age, I learned some pretty hard lessons about money. My mother raised my sister and me on a meagre salary, without any support from our father. I was well aware that my mother couldn't always pay the bills or put food on the table. I knew I wouldn't get expensive toys for Christmas, go on fancy summer vacations, or have the chance to attend that special gymnastics camp I so desperately wanted to go to. Although we weren't deprived in any way, in our house money was always an issue. As it turns out, it was also a great educator.

Watching my mom struggle taught me to work for what I wanted and to appreciate what I had. It taught me that money is not an excuse or a predictor of success. And it taught me that if I worked hard enough, I could not only survive, I could thrive. Despite not knowing what I would do after I left my job, I believed in my ability to figure it out. Remembering my childhood and recognizing the challenges I overcame throughout university, I also knew I could survive on a lot less money than I was making. Those strong beliefs gave me the courage I needed to walk away from that steady paycheck when I did.

Several of the FabFinders talked about events from their childhoods or comments from parents and role models that affected their decisions. A graphic designer remembered being diverted into engineering because her father thought she couldn't make a living with her artistic talents. An Internet marketer attributed his entrepreneurial drive to watching his parents; this formed his belief that owning your own business was the only true way to have control over your time, money, and legacy. A personal trainer told me that growing up with nothing caused him to believe that acquiring material stuff would make him happy.

It is beyond the scope of this book to analyze whether you have healthy values where money is concerned. However, heightening your awareness of what influenced those values can be very empowering. It means you can choose how it impacts your future actions, and you can intentionally shift your behaviour as appropriate. In my early career, I found a job that paid me substantially more money than my single mother ever made. Initially I loved the fact that I didn't have to stress about money the way my mom did. I never had to worry if I could pay the bills or afford to eat. Those things were very important to me. However, eventually I understood that I didn't need quite as much money as I was making in order to feel that way. I realized I'd rather make half the money if I could be twice as happy.

Consider your childhood and how money was introduced in your home. Think about the comments you overheard about how much money people make and what it means. Whether you watched your parents struggle or basked in the ignorance of how wealthy you were, it made an impact. Were you rich or poor? What effect did it have on your experiences and your happiness in general? Does the fear of lack of money, or the desire to live a certain way, prevent you from moving toward your version of a fabulous life?

Were you guided toward any particular job or career merely because of the potential salary? Are you letting those opinions limit your possibilities in terms of new jobs, careers, or lifestyles?

Comparative Analysis: "Keeping up with the Joneses"

> *Too many people spend money they earn, to buy things they don't want, to impress people they don't like.*
>
> **Will Rogers**

A friend of mine has a beautiful old home on a quiet suburban street, with the perfect number of bedrooms for her family's size. There's a nice backyard and mature trees that provide a warm, friendly environment for kids to play in. So what's wrong with it? If you ask me, I'd say nothing. I think it's perfect for them. However, I can hear the frustration in her voice as she tells me what her mother-in-law thinks. Apparently, she thinks their house is fine for a *starter* home, but she can't understand why they don't want to move to a bigger, brand-new home as soon as they can afford it. My friend and her husband have no interest in being mortgage poor, and prefer to spend their money on travelling and activities with their kids. They have a clear picture of what they want their lifestyle to be, and, quite admirably, ignore the opinion of others.

I find their example so remarkable because I think it is more common for people to be influenced by the views of society, friends, acquaintances, and even strangers. We let other people affect our perceptions of how much money we need, rather than taking the time to figure that out for ourselves. I was guilty of this for years. Any time I would confess my desire to leave, my colleagues would say, "Who else is going to pay us what we get paid?" How long did I let those kinds of comments hold me back? I wasn't worried about going hungry, so why did I think I had to make the same amount of money as anyone else?

When I asked the FabFinders about their early goals and the reasons they chose their careers, I often heard variations of, "I wanted the big salary, the fancy house, and the luxury car, just like everyone else." There seemed to be a sense of competition based on the comparison with what their friends and neighbours seemed to be acquiring. Money comparisons not only plagued their pasts, it also challenged their choices for a better future. One young woman who was ready to quit her job and chase her dreams spoke about feeling pressure from friends to start saving for a house and put money away for retirement. A marketing executive who was only a few years away from retirement recalled being conflicted when colleagues thought she was crazy to give up the nest egg of her pension to find fulfillment.

Of all the interviews I did, I think it was Katie's story that really drilled this point home for me. She was the one who showed me what happens when you choose to see other possibilities and stop trying to "keep up with the Joneses."

Katie's Story

For Katie, "'keeping up with the Joneses" meant she spent more than an hour each day in traffic, traveling twelve miles to her job as an elementary school teacher. Although she enjoyed teaching for the most part, the heavy traffic and long commute had her questioning her life. Why was she spending hours in the car in a state of frustration for a job that was just okay? Her longing to quit her job and go back to school to develop her artistic talents seemed unrealistic when she considered how she and her husband could get by on only his salary. Just like their friends and family, they had a large home with a mortgage and car payments.

It took a chance meeting with a charming family at a campground to change her thoughts about money.

After their families had spent some getting to know each other, Katie discovered that her new friends, a family of five, were living on a salary that was about a third of the income she and her husband would have if she quit her job. To her surprise, it seemed like this family was quite happy, travelling and enjoying their life. All of a sudden, Katie started to re-evaluate how much money her own family needed. Perhaps they could make it work if they made some changes to how they spent money and, more importantly, the way they thought about how much they needed to spend. Despite not knowing exactly how it would turn out, this change in perspective was what Katie needed to take her first leap of faith.

At the time of the interview, Katie had quit her teaching job and was designing her new career. She and her husband had downsized their home, adjusted their spending, and seemed to be happier than ever. In fact, she had just won second place in an art contest, earned a contract sketching for a biologist (with the potential to illustrate his upcoming book), and found a job teaching art at a local college. While she admits that she still worries about saving money for retirement since she left behind her teacher's pension, it seems that new opportunities present themselves every day. Concentrating on the small wins gives her the confidence and courage to keep moving toward her dreams. The more she does that, the more it seems the next step or opportunity just suddenly appears.

Noticing what others have can give you a sense of what is possible, and might even spark a new desire. Whether you see the chance for more happiness or more financial wealth, recognizing new possibilities can put you on a new course. However, constantly comparing your life to others' and competing with someone else is a losing battle—a message I heard many times during the interviews. Katie and her husband realized they had been determining their financial needs by comparing themselves to their friends and neighbours. Meeting the family of five gave them a new perspective on the cost of happiness.

The things that make Katie happy and fit her definition of fabulous may not be the same for you or me. External displays of happiness or success may not accurately reflect internal thoughts and feelings. Mine certainly didn't. Do you think people could have seen me in my company car, filling up with the company gas card, and driving to my lake front cottage as clues to my unhappiness and lack of fulfillment? For me, owning a cottage brings me joy, but not for the reason it might bring others. I love the time and space to enjoy my friends and family and the connection I feel with nature. It has nothing to do with acquiring assets so I can seem richer than I feel. I would have given up that cottage in a heartbeat if I had been able to exchange it for true fulfillment and a sense of purpose.

Judging someone else's happiness based on the money they have (or the things money buys) is just as meaningless as other people judging *your* happiness based on what you have or don't have. Only you can do that. The lesson here is simple: clarify and own your values relating to money. I don't believe there is anything wrong with wanting a lot of it, but want it for *you*, not because of someone else. Once you are clear and confident about what determines Fabulous for you, it frees you from the comparison game.

Neighbours with fancy cars and friends with the latest electronics or memberships to exclusive clubs can influence your thoughts about what you think you want. Again, there is nothing wrong with wanting these things as long as you are clear on *why* you want them. Are external pressures determining how much money you think you want or need?

There is a difference between seeing possibility and competing. Are you just trying to "*keep up with the Joneses*"? Are you letting *their* idea of fabulous hold you back from investing in *yours*?

Debts & Obligations

You must gain control over your money or the lack of it will forever control you.

Dave Ramsey

How does a stressed-out, overweight smoker dig himself out of debt, turn his health around, quit his job, and still find a way to provide for his family of eight? One of the best examples I came across during my research was the story of Leo Babauta. His is perhaps the best real-life example I could offer to illustrate how family obligations and even severe debt don't have to hold you back from pursuing your dreams. In fact, in Leo's case you could almost say it was the prerequisite for discovering his version of Fabulous.

An initial decision to quit smoking and start exercising turned into a life purpose as Leo slowly turned his life around. Sharing how he was able to make huge strides with small steps, Leo created *Zen Habits,* which has become one of the world's top blogs and websites. He was able to simplify his life, get himself out of debt, and create a lucrative business for himself in the process. The popularity of his blog and best-selling books eventually allowed

Leo to quit his full-time job and move his family from Guam to San Francisco. Among many other life-changing consequences, this has enabled Leo to support his family while working a fraction of the time he did before.

People often tell me the decision to leave the security of my steady salary behind was only possible because I didn't have children. I hate that comment! How do they know what I would or would not have done? Although I recognize having children may have changed the course and perhaps the timing of my journey, I honestly don't think it would have stopped me. Since I can't possibly know that for sure, I intentionally searched out FabFinders with kids. I didn't want to presume I understood anything about Finding Fabulous while raising one child, much less a brood the size of Leo's!

I hope Leo's story provides you with hope and the inspiration that, regardless of your debts and obligations, it is possible to find or design your dream job and lifestyle. His story isn't the only one. In fact, the majority of the FabFinders I spoke to had families with children of varying ages.

I met Mikey early in my journey. I was quickly impressed with (and equally curious to learn about) how, with a wife and four kids at home, he was able to walk away from his six-figure salary. His story is a great lesson in the power of planning and a fantastic example of a phased approached to transformational shifts.

Mikey's Story

> *How does a forty-year-old man with four children and a wife to support walk away from his role as the National Director of HR at an IT company to become an entertainer, speaker, and trainer? It would take a little soul-searching and a lot of planning, but Mikey did just that.*
>
> *Despite finally hitting the salary level and earning the benefits he had always dreamed of, Mikey knew that working in HR was not his passion. "No amount of money was going to cure my 'I hate my job sickness'," he says. He remembers days when it had gotten so bad that he would close the door to his office and just cry.*

His "ah-ha" moment came one day when he was speaking to his ten-year-old daughter on the phone. "Daddy, you sound bored," she said. Thinking about how hard he had been working to mask his unhappiness, he suddenly realized how much it was affecting his home life. That discovery, oddly, made him feel free.

Immediately after hanging up the phone, Mikey started to write in his journal. He asked himself, "Who am I? What am I? Is this what I want to be doing? What is my calling and purpose in life? What makes me come alive?" He spent the next six months soul searching, looking for the answers to those questions. Eventually he came up with a plan to become a corporate trainer, keynote speaker, and comedy entertainer. Unable to quit his job right away, Mikey built a strategic exit plan that would allow him to follow his passion and still feed his family.

In order to get a sense for whether he could make a living as an entertainer, Mikey started to study hypnosis and performing while he continued to work for the IT firm. Gaining self-confidence from a show he did for five hundred high school students, Mikey realized he could do anything he set his mind to. Building on that confidence, he did a handful of fairs and a few more high schools, and soon he was able to secure an agent. With that part of his plan in place, Mikey attacked the idea of being a corporate trainer; leveraging the one skill set he actually enjoyed using in his HR role, he was able to land a contract with a corporate training firm.

With that contract lined up, and several entertaining gigs planned, Mikey took what he calls a "calculated risk" and finally quit his job. Being an author and speaker formed the third tier of his plan, which he was able to work on after he quit his day job. Although he admits his biggest challenge has been financial, he attributes his success to having a laser focus on his goals. First and foremost, he wants to pursue his passion, and he sees money as just a by-product of those dreams.

> *At the age of 43, he has recently published his first book, and he's already checked off most of the items on his bucket list. Summing up the value of money in his life, he says, "I have a great family, a beautiful home and get to follow my passions. The rest is just gravy."*

Both Mikey and Leo had to do a lot of planning and saving before they were able to walk away from their day jobs. My path was very different. Financially, I had a buffer. Aside from not having the obligations of children, years of saving and investing, combined with a healthy severance package, afforded me some time. Other than my mortgage, I wasn't in debt. My situation afforded me the benefit of being able to leave my job without having to take on another one right away. Nevertheless, I still had to plan for my cost of living and adjust my spending accordingly.

There is no right, wrong, or even ideal financial path to Finding Fabulous—only the one that fits your situation. Some FabFinders started to build their new businesses in their spare time while they kept their day jobs. The law clerk who discovered network marketing was eventually able to decrease her day job hours as her new business gained traction and started to earn additional income. One couple chose to decrease their spending drastically, freeing themselves from financial obligations in order to buy some time after they simultaneously chose to leave their jobs behind. Beena's path was sort of a combination of mine, Jess's, and Mikey's. Initially she was able to live off her savings after she left marketing to create a coaching business. Eventually she accepted a job with another organization to supplement her income while she continued to work on growing her business. The new job was better aligned to her dream job than marketing had been, giving her valuable experience while allowing her to build her business on the side.

If you are bogged down with credit card debt and barely able to pay rent or put food on the table, then your path to *Finding Fabulous* will look different from mine. Your specific situation will determine the path you choose, but that doesn't have to limit your ability to start. Your first steps may center on decreasing that debt and controlling your spending while you work on figuring out your next move. Maybe, like Mikey and Leo, you have to start planning a phased exit strategy or, like Jess and Beena, you may need to consider supplemental income sources. Taking the time to clarify your financial obligations can determine whether money is a major roadblock or simply a manageable hurdle on your path to *Finding Fabulous*.

What are your debts and obligations? Are you swimming in debt? Do you have savings that could offer a buffer? Does anyone else rely on you for financial support? Have you been using those obligations as an excuse for not taking action toward living your dreams?

Want vs. Need

> *Wealth consists not in having great possessions,*
> *but in having few wants.*
>
> **Epictetus**

"Ah, the difference between need and want—such a fuzzy line!" That's an expression I used to favour whenever I was shopping with a girlfriend. Whether she was arguing the practicality of a little black dress, evaluating the purchase of both pairs of new shoes, or justifying the use of a maxed-out credit card, I found humour in the debate. It seems the term "need" can be argued either way. Back then I was working that lucrative job and had the disposable income to make the point rather moot. But is it a moot point? Does it matter if we buy things we don't need, or even necessarily want, if we have the money to do it?

There's nothing like a fixed income to bring that debate to a close! Growing up with no money gave me enough ambition to get to the point where money didn't control my choices. I didn't have to decline a night out with friends, walk away from that new outfit, or turn down an opportunity to travel because my paycheck was overspent. Luckily for me, I could afford most of the things I wanted. However, I was so busy not worrying about money that I didn't realize I was buying things I didn't even want, let alone need!

If you have the opportunity to read Leo Babauta's full story (you can find it on his website at www.zenhabits.net), you'll learn that, although he believes that many things contributed to his success, it started with becoming more frugal and getting himself out of debt. He didn't stop there, though; he intentionally chose to reduce a lot of "clutter" (as he calls it) and to adopt a simpler lifestyle. In essence, he redefined what he needed, what he wanted, and what he could do without. He goes into more specifics on his blog, listing things like cutting cable TV, not eating out or going to the movies, and only buying new clothes when essential. These are principles he still follows today, despite being debt-free.

Although I don't think everyone has to become as frugal as Leo, I do think his example highlights an important point. I like to think *Finding Fabulous*, in terms of spending money, comes down to a simple equation:

$$(Need) + (Want) - (Everything\ Else)$$

Figure out the cost of your needs and the amount of your wants, and be willing to give up everything else. Throw in a sense of how much time it will take you to find and start living that fabulous life, and you have the solution!

What's your equation? If you have ever used the excuse, "I can't afford to go after my dreams," in any form or fashion, I'll ask you, "Have you done the math?" Are you clear about what you want, what you need, and everything else that currently drains your financial resources? Do you know how much needs to be written on that fictitious dream-finding check in order to get started?

Need: What do you really need?

Living on a fixed income has helped me decide between what I really want and what I need. Since I'm on the path to Finding Fabulous, I'm not in the mindset of depriving myself of life's pleasures. However, as I mentioned, I've come to realize that over the years I got into the habit of spending money on a lot of things I didn't really want or need. My current situation has given me new perspective on where my money goes. For instance, my home telephone bill used to cost more than fifty dollars a month. I live alone and I also have a cell phone. Why do I need a home phone? Couple that question with the fact that the majority of calls to my home phone are from telemarketers, and the decision becomes quite simple. I don't need or want a home phone. Taking the same approach with my satellite TV, I realized I didn't need all the channels I was paying for, so I cut that back with no consequence. Combining the savings from the two, I now need to earn $110 less per month. I didn't give up anything I wanted; I just clarified what I needed.

The process of understanding what you need does not have to be a painful one. You don't necessarily have to give up the things you want. We'll discuss the decision to temporarily give up some of those things, if it's necessary, in the section on willingness, but for now let's concentrate on the difference it can make.

Which of your current expenses are for things you really need? Could the cost of those things be reduced without affecting your lifestyle (e.g., decreasing the cost of your phone/cell bill or even downsizing your home and mortgage)?

Want: What is it that you really want?

It could be debated that our society is full of people who have more things than they really need. I believe it could also be said that we don't understand the things we really want. Could our surroundings and current perception of what's realistic be limiting our awareness of possibilities?

For me, understanding what I really want has been a process. It didn't come naturally. As I invested time and effort into uncovering what I really want for my life, I started to discover things I had never considered. For example, I didn't know I could make a living remotely. I've always gotten a lot of pleasure out of traveling, but I always thought that was something you do for vacation. Even though I was fortunate enough to travel to some amazing countries for work, corporate travel was exhausting, and the schedules were too tight to fully explore my surroundings. Thinking vacation time was the only way I could travel at my own pace, I used to want more vacation and the money to pay for it. But what would that have really given me? Often, I would return from vacation to a full inbox and voice mail requests, replacing all the stress I had just relieved on the vacation. Wouldn't one or two more weeks of vacation just repeat that cycle?

it a flexible schedule and passive income sources that allow me to ⟨...⟩tely while I travel the world. I want my physical surroundings to blur the lines between work and play. I didn't know these possibilities existed until I met some of the FabFinders. Research for this book has taught me so much about possibilities; in turn, I've redefined what I want.

What do you really want? As you do the math to figure out how much money you require, consider the type of lifestyle and experiences you want in addition to material things.

Other: Everything else

> *A house is just a place to keep your stuff while you go out and get more stuff.*
>
> **George Carlin**

My previous career required me to move quite frequently. I was open to exploring new cities and got use to packing up my belongings and living out of boxes as the situation demanded. One particular move provided an interesting exercise in determining what I didn't really need or want. This move required me to store the majority of my belongings for a period of about four months, and when I was finally settled in my new home, the moving truck brought back all of my *stuff*. I had survived for months without many of those things. Of course, storing summer clothes during winter turned out to be a bad idea when I made a last-minute decision to fly south for a week, but the majority of the things had gone unmissed. As I started to unpack boxes, I came across a few that I hadn't opened during my two or three previous moves. What on earth could I have needed in those boxes? I made a bold decision and tossed one of them without even opening it! Crazy? Maybe. But it was also liberating.

This idea of re-evaluating things that were neither wanted nor needed was not unique to me. Several of the FabFinders seemed to go through the same process. Perhaps the journey of *Finding Fabulous* carries with it the side effect of detachment. I cared so much less about my *stuff* once I realized that I wanted different *experiences*. One couple agreed with me as they explained the impact of simplifying their lives. They believe that downsizing their home has actually created more space and energy in their lives. They want fewer things and feel they don't need that much to be happy.

Shannon and Andy were another couple who agreed with this philosophy, offering perhaps the most extreme example of clearing your life of things you no longer want or need. Although not all of us would be comfortable with the lifestyle that grew from their choices, I think we can all learn something from this amazing couple.

Shannon & Andy

When I first met Shannon and Andy, they were on a journey, one that started with selling most of their belongings, packing their dog in the car, and heading west. They had become disheartened with their work and where their lives were in general, and so started a journey that would take them to Western Canada, across the United States, around Europe, and eventually back home.

Although friends questioned their newly adopted, somewhat nomadic lifestyle, that year of travel gave them new perspective on what they thought of the world and what was most important to them. It was perhaps the time spent in a retirement community in Florida which provided the validation that they were on the right path. Contrary to the opinions of friends their own age who thought they should be buying a house and saving for retirement, the older retirees thought their actions were admirable and brave.

Reflecting on that experience, Shannon explains, "Everyone who is working is waiting until retirement to truly live, and everyone in retirement is wishing they hadn't waited so long to do the things they love."

Looking for insights into how a couple could survive as long as they have without either of them earning an income, I asked them the money question. They offered this advice for others: "Before making a major career shift, consider decreasing your debts and your cost of living. Get really clear on what you need versus what you want. By getting rid of extra costs, you won't need as much money every month, and therefore will have more flexibility while you figure out where your income will come from, or when your new venture will start paying off."

For this couple, they followed their own advice for a year while they planned to make a big change. They had enough insight to know it might take a while to figure it out, and they were willing to do what it takes, living more simply as they endeavoured to find their version of fabulous. They got rid of their monthly cell phone bills by switching to pay-as-you-go plans. This not only gave them more flexibility to adjust the expense up or down as required, it also meant they weren't committed to a contract. As it turned out, living on a tight budget—decreasing their spending and lightening their lives of extraneous material things—reinforced how irrelevant those things were to their happiness.

In the end, that year of travel and self-discovery clarified for Shannon and Andy the values that would guide their decisions moving forward. Although their first few attempts as entrepreneurs didn't take off the way they had originally hoped, they learned a lot in the process. Their ventures included owning their own web design company, manufacturing a line of pet clothing, and eventually starting a satirical comic strip business. Each business idea took them closer to what they want to do with their lives, and the ups and downs along the way taught them who they want to be.

Although many people may not be willing to go to the extremes that this couple did, their path to *Finding Fabulous* is a great example that proves you can find the money necessary to make a career shift by simply changing how you think about it and the way you spend it.

So what does that full equation look like for you?

Cost of Finding Fabulous =

Cost of <u>Needs</u> + Cost of <u>Wants</u> − Cost of <u>Everything</u>

Could doing the math and clarifying the full picture help redefine what is possible for your journey of *Finding Fabulous*?

Willingness

What impacts our willingness to do what it takes?

Whether or not you knew the exact amount of money to ask for on that check I offered you earlier, I bet you liked the idea. Wanting more money is the easy part. Perhaps more difficult is determining what you are willing to do, give, or be in order to acquire that money. Finding Fabulous isn't all that different; you still have to know how willing you are to do what it takes to find it.

When I first started in the pharmaceutical industry, my company's head office was based in Toronto. I remember talking with the other reps in my training class about how fun it would be to live in Toronto and work at the company's headquarters. However, before I reached that place in my career, the company merged with one based in Montreal. All of a sudden, those same sales reps weren't interested in any career advancement that meant moving out of province or learning French. That unwillingness to relocate limited their options. For me, the opportunity to take on more responsibility, learn new roles, and earn a higher income trumped the negatives of having to move, so I did. Years later, after moving back to my home province, I had to contemplate my willingness to go back to Montreal. The company was going through another downsizing, and opportunities were sparse. This time, I wasn't as willing to move. In fact, as you know, I wasn't even willing to stay with the company.

The final decision to look for work that had more purpose and meaning for me meant that I had to be willing to face something more uncomfortable than moving to a new city: uncertainty. I had to be willing to not have all the answers. I had to be willing to do the work to reinvent (or rediscover) myself. I had to be willing to dip into my savings, to give up my company car, and to go without medical benefits and the many other perks of the job. Every day since that decision has been a lesson in determining what I'm willing to do to continue living the life of my dreams.

The FabFinders and I had this in common. I think about Jacqueline, who had to be willing to downsize her home and move her child to another school so she could leave her law practice behind. I'm reminded of two of my close friends who had to be willing to drain their bank accounts and retirement savings plans in order to support themselves while they designed their ideal lives. And of course we've already discussed Shannon and Andy's willingness to sell almost everything they owned!

Everyone has a different idea of what they are and are not willing to exchange for *Finding Fabulous*. Since those things are often tied to money, it warrants discussing here. Without judging anyone's willingness or lack thereof, I came to understand three key areas that seemed to differentiate the FabFinders' willingness from that of others I met along the way.

1. **Perception of Risk**—The illusion of security & danger of "what if"

2. **Loss vs. Investment**—The possibility of something better

3. **Timing**—The time it will take to start making money again

Perception of Risk

What if I told you that you could have everything you ever dreamed of, but you would have to risk everything you have in order to get it? Would you be willing to take the risk? There are some people who would jump at that chance, while many others would shrink in fear of it. Why is that? Which one are you? Which part of the sentence drew more of your attention? Did you hear the part about getting everything you ever wanted, or were you too focused on the part about risking everything you have?

Recently, I was having a conversation with a friend of mine about daring to go after dreams when he quoted the old saying, "a bird in the hand is worth two in the bush," as a practical reason for why people settle. It got me thinking about how people perceive risk. The guaranteed "bird in the hand" sounds pretty good unless you realize it's not the kind of "bird" you worth risking the one, even if you aren't completely certain you c other two?

The FabFinders were not strangers to taking risks. When I walked away from my corporate stability, I risked not being able to find work doing what I loved. When Chris walked away from a potential partnership at the consulting firm, he risked never being able to make it as an entrepreneur. Shelagh risked the financial security of a teacher's pension as she dared to open her own business. Each of them knew what they were risking and, more importantly, what they could possibly gain.

In his now-famous commencement speech at the Maharishi University of Management, Jim Carrey summed up this lesson beautifully:

> *So many of us choose our path out of fear, disguised as practicality. What we really want seems impossibly out of reach and ridiculous to expect, so we never dare to ask the universe for it. I'm saying I'm the proof that you can ask the universe for it ...*
>
> *My father could have been a great comedian, but he didn't believe that that was possible for him. So he made a conservative choice and instead he got a safe job as an accountant. And, when I was twelve years old, he was let go from that safe job, and our family had to do whatever we could to survive. I learned many great lessons from my father, not the least of which is that you can fail at what you don't want, so you might as well take a chance at doing what you love.*

Jim Carrey raises a great point about perception of risk. Often people think staying in a "stable" job is a safer option than taking the leap toward what they really want. But is the risk any less, or is it just an illusion of safety?

Our FabFinder Angela found the answer: a year after she walked away from her "stable" sales job, it was eliminated. If she had stayed with the global, seemingly safe company, she would have been out of a job. Had I made it through the downsizing that was going on at my company when I chose to leave, I may have been let go a year later when they went through additional cuts. Even though I also worked for a large global organization that appeared to be around for the long haul, there were no guarantees.

So why don't more people dare to do what they love? Why do people perceive the risk of leaving a stable job is any greater than staying? After years of speaking to people about this topic, I have come to believe that, more often than not, the focus is on the potential pitfalls rather than the possible gains. I think we are programmed to "what if" our options in favor of the negative possibilities.

> What if I can't find a job? What if I lose my house because I can't pay my bills? What if no one wants what I have to offer?

Not that those things aren't valid concerns, but take a moment to consider the "*two in the bush*" angle of that discussion.

> What if I find a job that I love twice as much? What if I make more money than I ever imagined and pay off my mortgage twice as quickly? What if my offering is so important that it could change people's lives for the better?

Are the positive "what ifs" any less likely to happen than the negative ones? If you actively work towards the positive side, and there is no reason to think anyone would be actively working against you, isn't it reasonable to think the scales would tip in your favour?

In recognition of the anxieties that come with taking risks and going after your dreams, the FabFinders offered some advice. Many of them suggested that people plan for potential disasters ahead of time. One entrepreneur advised that people figure out how much money they need, and double that amount. That way, they can focus on growing their business and offering value rather than wasting energy on financial concerns. Mikey's example demonstrated how diversifying and phasing in future income can protect against some of those negative "what ifs." What if he wasn't able to get entertainment gigs? He had a training job to get him by. What if his family couldn't tolerate the travel associated with the training? He had passive income plans with the publishing of his new book.

Planning ahead for disasters puts them into perspective. For example, what if you can't find a job? If this is a possibility, consider how long you could manage without one. Prepare ahead for that amount of time to relieve some of the stress. The idea is to *Find Fabulous*, even if the journey might at times be uncomfortable. Planning for some of that discomfort not only better prepares you, but it also quiets the anxiety. Shifting from disaster mode to solution mode can be very empowering. It allows you to have options for your worst-case scenarios while keeping it all in perspective.

Are you letting your perceptions of risk affect your willingness to go after your dreams? Could you "what if" the positives in an effort to bring more perspective to your options?

Loss vs. Investment

Consider again that offer to have everything you ever dreamed of, but having to risk what you have now. If you could know ahead of time what you risked or gave up would only be temporary, would that change your willingness to do what it takes? What if you would lose what you had, but would gain something better? Would that change your willingness?

Many of the FabFinders were faced with the dilemma of what they were willing to give up if they chose to go after their dreams. Jacqueline was one of those FabFinders. Her story illustrates how giving up something can actually be an investment toward something better.

Jacqueline's Story

Jacqueline hadn't slept well in nearly eight years! Assuming her insomnia was a normal side effect after giving birth, she never stopped to consider what else might be causing it. It wasn't until a skiing accident left her temporarily unable to walk and permanently unable to ski that she started to evaluate her life.

Despite having been a successful insurance lawyer for twelve years, Jacqueline was miserable. She couldn't even remember why she went into law in the first place. However, the large home, elaborate vacations, and designer handbags that filled her closets had somewhat compensated for the stress, anxiety, and unhappiness she felt. After the skiing accident, she realized she was working in a job that made her miserable in order to afford luxuries she might not be able to enjoy.

The thought of leaving her law practice to pursue another career was not exactly a comfortable one. Since she was the family's major breadwinner, Jacqueline's decision meant they would have to sell their beautiful home, move to another neighbourhood, and enrol their daughter in a new school. Despite how uncomfortable that was for her, she was lucky enough to have a husband who wanted her happiness more than her salary. The major cut in their household income meant they needed to learn how to budget and redefine what they really needed to be happy.

Only a few short months after making the switch from law to a marketing and communications job, Jacqueline has already discovered that she doesn't need or want all the material stuff she used to buy. Reflecting on those expensive designer handbags she still owns, she believes that even if she can afford them again one day, she's not sure she'd want them. Loving her new job and sleeping soundly at night for the first time in eight years, she knows she made the right choice for herself and her family.

She summed it up nicely by saying, "It doesn't always feel brave, but I know what it means for my daughter to see her mom happy."

Changing perspective from loss to exchange allowed Jacqueline to explore more options. Instead of being trapped by her situation, she could view the things in her life as assets that could be leveraged toward a more fabulous life.

As you consider what you are and are not willing to give up in order to pursue your fabulous life, remember this technique as a way to filter your decisions. What would you lose if you went after your dreams? Would you be more willing to exchange or "invest" those things in order to live a fuller life?

Timing is Everything

Imagine for a moment that you're at a carnival. There is a coloured tent with a table inside, draped with a velvet cloth. As you get closer, you notice a shiny crystal ball perched on top of the table. What if you could use that magic ball to see into the future and know for certain whether you would be successful in accomplishing your dreams? Would you want to know that? Before you answer, let me tell you that the crystal ball isn't great at understanding the dimension of time. It may indeed know that you will have everything you ever imagine, but it's not sure if it will take five, ten, or even twenty years to get it. Does that change your mind?

Each year for several years after starting my career, I contemplated going back to medical school. I would consider how long the process would take and how old I would be when I finally graduated and started making money. Inevitably I would conclude that I was too old and it would take too long. I wasn't willing to put in the time to accomplish that dream. A funny thing would happen the following year: I would go through the exact same process, only this time I'd regret not having taken steps the year before.

Going after your dreams takes time. Unfortunately, since I don't have a crystal ball, I have no idea how long it will take you to get what you want. What I do know for sure is that the time it will take won't start ticking until the first day you decide to act. That means if you hesitate one day, a five-year dream will take five years plus one day. It means if you wait one year to start, a ten-year dream will take eleven years to acquire, and so on. Are you willing to put in the time? Are you willing to start now, even though you might not see the fruits of your labor for years?

As we discussed in the debts and obligations section, timing is another factor to consider where money is concerned. Doing the work to estimate the time for your path can help you plan financially and otherwise. Although I can't guarantee that reading this book will shorten your path, I do believe the FabFinders offer some great advice about planning for whatever length of time it takes. If nothing else, I hope their stories inspire you to start now!

Some of the *FabFinders* were able to quit their jobs immediately, while others needed to plan for years before taking the leap. In order to shorten the time it would take to build his dream, a personal trainer chose to work eighty-hour weeks, saving money while simultaneously starting construction on his own gym. He was willing to sacrifice his time to make it happen. Mikey's exit strategy took eighteen months to plan and a willingness to stick with his HR job in the meantime. Chris had a severance package that allowed him to start his business immediately, with a buffer to support his family until he started making money. I hope you can appreciate that there are many paths to achieving what you seek. A challenge with money doesn't have to limit your dreams; it may just dictate the timing.

When I met Martin, he put all of my decisions and lack of action to shame. Martin is a great example of what can happen if you are willing to put in the time.

Martin's Story

> *Martin was a well-respected police officer before he found his calling to become a family physician. Even though he had risen through the police ranks relatively quickly, his longing to serve people was not fully being met. Since he had become a cop straight out of high school, he lacked the undergraduate degree required to apply to medical school. Having to support a wife and new baby at the time, he was unable to leave his job, so he chose to carry a full university course load while continuing to work full-time hours.*

> *When I asked him how he had the motivation to endure the long hours and lack of sleep, he told me how clearly he saw his end goal, and he knew the kind of role model he wanted to be for his daughter. "I wanted to show her that it is never too late to go after your dreams," he says proudly.*

> *Doing his daughter proud, and to the benefit of hundreds of patients, Martin exemplifies how a person's situation doesn't have to dictate his future possibilities. In his path to Finding Fabulous,*

Martin has shown us how a willingness to endure short-term pain can result in long-term gain.

Going back to school full-time while continuing to work full-time hours, along with raising a toddler, have to win the prize for effort! I like to keep Martin's commitment in mind any time I think I don't have the time or effort to make my dreams come true.

Martin and other FabFinders offered several pieces of advice on the topic of money, including the suggestion that people don't leap without looking. If you are buried in debt, unable to pay your bills, and struggling to stay afloat, it might not be a great time to quit your job without having something to replace the income. Martin worked and went to school in his preparation. Angela attended weekend personal growth seminars while she kept her day job. In other words, timing is key, but it doesn't mean delay. Don't delay your dream because you can't quit right away. Start planning, doing, dreaming, or whatever it takes to make those first critical steps.

The degree of clarity you have about what you want, combined with a realistic evaluation of your current financial situation, allows you to plan the timing accordingly. Consider all the factors we've listed above (beliefs about money, want vs. need, debts and obligations, risk tolerance, and willingness) to determine the perfect timing for you.

Roadmap: Show Me the Money

Now it's your turn. Are you letting money get in your way? If so, let's do some work to uncover which aspects of money are holding you back or slowing your progress the most.

- **Key Influencers**—Are you letting others influence your ideas about how much money you need to have or make?
- **Want vs. Need**—Do you have a clear understanding of what you need versus what you want?
- **Willingness**—What factors determine what you are and aren't willing to do in order to find your version of fabulous?

Remember, this is a journey of finding _fabulous_. Although it is realistic to expect the journey to be challenging and uncomfortable at times, it isn't meant to be painful or depriving. The examples and suggestions provided here are not meant as the be-all, end-all solutions for any one person. If they don't fit with your life, or they feel too depriving, don't employ them. The purpose of this chapter is to raise your awareness and challenge how you think about money. Be creative and come up with your own solutions. Just remember that investing time to understand how you think, feel, and act with respect to money will get you that much closer to _Finding Fabulous_.

Key Influencers – What You Think about Money and Why

Understanding why you think you need or want a certain amount of money can help guide your actions accordingly.

Past Experiences: How have your past experiences affected your decisions?

My desire to make a lot of money was more about control over my bills and freedom to do the things I wanted. With more introspection, I realized money could only help to a point, and I re-evaluated how much I truly needed.

Is money a key driver or definition of success for you?

- ☐ What preconceived ideas do you have about money? How are they limiting your perception of career options available to you?
- ☐ List all the reasons for your career choices up to this point. How many of those reasons are tied to money in some way?
- ☐ Whether you want to be financially rich or not, write down a salary range that you would be comfortable with. (You don't have to know the exact amount. At this point we are just getting an overall picture of your thoughts.)

Comparative Analysis: Are you trying to compete with others?

Katie and her husband realized they could get by living on a lot less income if they stopped trying to keep up with friends and neighbours. Downsizing their home and adjusting their spending gave Katie the freedom to pursue her art career.

- ☐ Do you feel acceptance from friends, family, or society is tied to how much money you have or how much you make?
- ☐ Think about the large purchases you have made over the past several years. Ignoring what other people around you may or may not have, how many of those purchases were the right decision for you and your family?

Debts & Obligations: Who is relying on you?

Leo not only got himself out of debt, he also designed a new way of life and a career that allows him to provide for his large family. Mikey was strategic in building an eighteen-month exit strategy so he could leave his day job and still raise four kids. Both of them provide proof that it can be done.

- ☐ Are you using your debts as a reason for not pursuing your dreams?

    If so, start making a plan to turn your financial situation around. Try one of these options:

- ✓ Hire a debt counsellor or financial planner.
- ✓ Look into debt forgiveness or consolidation options.
- ✓ Get serious about decreasing your weekly spending
- ✓ Read Leo Babauta's blog *Zen Habits* for more examples of how he got himself out of debt.

☐ Do you believe obligations like children, spouses, or parents make pursuing your dreams unrealistic?

If so, ask yourself if the cost of supporting your dependents is the main issue (compared to your lack of time, support, energy, etc.)

- ✓ If money really is the issue, consider Mikey & Leo's examples.
- ✓ Design a phased plan to decrease your expenditures.
- ✓ Start your new business on the side while keeping your day job.
- ✓ Consider ways you can supplement your income (e.g., real estate investments, selling products online, network marketing, etc.)

Want vs. Need – How Much Do You Really Need?

Don't just think about whether you can afford to go after your dreams or not, do the math! Get a clear picture of where you are currently spending your financial resources and re-evaluate your Cost of Finding Fabulous Equation.

$$\text{Cost of Finding Fabulous} = $$
$$\text{Cost of Needs} + \text{Cost of Wants} - \text{Cost of Everything Else}$$

Need, Want, or Other

Do you take the time to contemplate what you want, or is it something that you allow to happen as you go? Each time I moved my belongings, I found more and more stuff I didn't need or want. Re-evaluating the difference allowed me to gain new perspective on what my life could look like if I spent my money differently.

- ☐ Make a comprehensive list of all the things you spend money on each week, month, or year.
- ☐ Beside each item listed, mark whether you feel it is a "need," "want," or "other."

Cost of Finding Fabulous

Shannon and Andy were able to support themselves without an income for more than a year, based simply on the reduction in their cost of living. How much could you reduce your cost of living? What would you be willing to get rid of, either permanently or temporarily?

- ☐ Beside each item marked "need," consider whether you could decrease the cost of this obligation.
  - ✓ For each item you would be willing to reduce, write down the reduced amount.
  - ✓ Don't forget to consider things like mortgages and car loans if you are willing to downsize in your effort to follow your dreams.
- ☐ Beside each item marked "want," consider whether you would be willing to temporarily give this up in the pursuit of your dreams.
  - ✓ For items you are willing to give up temporarily, mark the cost down to zero.
  - ✓ Leave the other "wants" on your list for now, or decrease the amounts if appropriate.
- ☐ Beside each item marked "other," consider why you have been spending money on this item and make a final decision on whether you can remove it.
  - ✓ For items you are comfortable getting rid of, mark the cost down to zero.
  - ✓ For items you want to keep on the list, move them to either the "need" or "want" category.

- ☐ Add up all the amounts (reduced cost of needs + reduced cost of wants + new value of other).
  - ✓ Put the amount of money into a time frame based on how much money you need to live each week or month.

When you consider what you want, do you consider intangibles like experiences, lifestyle, and mindset along with tangible, material things?

- ☐ Make note of all the "nonmaterial" things you want for your life, including any lifestyle choices and experiences that will affect your financial situation (like living abroad, travelling frequently, becoming an entrepreneur, etc.)
  - ✓ Consider how those things could affect your finances.

Timing

Martin wasn't able to afford to quit his job as a police officer while he went back to school to earn a degree, so he continued to work full-time. Mikey phased his exit strategy over eighteen months, and Andy and Shannon took more than a year to save up for their transformation.

- ☐ How long do you need to save before making a move? How long would your savings sustain your lifestyle if it took you a while to earn money?
  - ✓ Consider the cost of living you calculated above and multiply it by the number of months you believe it will take before you are earning an income again.
- ☐ Would making some changes to your spending buy you more time?
- ☐ Is there anything else (special occasions, events, birth of a child, etc.) that might impact your timing?

Willingness – What are you willing to do?

Sometimes we have to be willing to make sacrifices to get where we want to go, or temporarily give up things we have in order to have something better. When I wanted to further my career in the corporate world, I was willing to move to a new province to accept the opportunities that were available.

Martin was willing to give up sleep while he worked and studied in order to become a physician. Jacqueline was willing to downsize her home, give up her expensive handbags, and move her daughter to a new school.

Would you be willing to do something similar or something short-term as you continue to find or create the lifestyle you want?

☐   What are some options if that happens?

☐   In a worst-case scenario, what would be your backup plan?

Chapter 5: Support

*It is a fact that in the right formation, the lifting power
of many wings can achieve twice the distance
of any bird flying alone.*

Author Unknown

In the film industry, movie stars get all the attention and most of the credit. Whether a movie is good or bad, a hit or a flop, the actors usually stand to inherit the accolades or are burdened with the rotten tomato reviews. However, whether they give Oscar-winning performances or break box office records, movie stars don't do it alone; they have an entire support team behind them. They might have an acting coach helping them refine their talent, a casting agent working hard to help them land the best roles, and an entire fan base cheering them on. Makeup artists give them just the right coloring, the lighting crew creates the best ambiance, and the cameramen capture their best angles. Not to mention the director, producer, and supporting actors who contribute to the success of a film. I think you get the idea: success is a team effort.

Consider for a moment that *Finding Fabulous* is a movie instead of your life. Who would you want supporting you in the production? Pretend you are the producer of this major motion picture. You have all sorts of resources at your disposal, and you can pick the best of the best. How cool would that be? I'm talking carte blanche! You could have Tony Robbins as a speaking coach, Kevin O'Leary as a business advisor, and even Steve Jobs as head of your innovation team. You could choose the happiest, most optimistic person you know to be your perpetual cheerleader and the smartest person you know to give you continual advice. There could be website experts, brilliant accountants, and even Ivy League professors who are experts in your subject matter. Who would you choose? If you were given full access to all the resources in the world, who would be on your *Finding Fabulous* team? What would create that ripple effect or tipping point that would take you from unrealized potential to ultimate success?

If you have clear answers to those questions, you are a lot closer to *Finding Fabulous* than I was when I started. Not only did I not know who I wanted on my team, I didn't even know I needed one! I knew that finding my passion and designing my fabulous life would take a lot of personal insight and a great deal of work. What I didn't fully appreciate was how important other people would be in that process. After all, if I didn't know what I wanted, how could someone else? If I couldn't describe what was blocking my progress, how could anyone help me remove those blocks? If I didn't know where the path led, how could I ask someone to help me get there?

When I walked away from that six-figure salary, full benefits, stock options, and a lucrative pension, some people thought I was crazy. Others thought I was brave. Some probably thought I was both! But I was so unhappy in my situation, and so ready to change, that I didn't care what anybody thought. I admit that the comments and quizzical stares initially frustrated me, but I knew I wouldn't get anywhere worrying about the opinions of others. At the same time, I quickly learned I'd have to be more intentional about who I spent my time with. I knew that hanging around people who inspired me to go after my dreams was much more productive (and fun) than trying to explain why I was doing it to the sceptics. It took me a little longer to grasp just how much support I needed. I had to figure out what type of support I needed, when it would be most beneficial, and where to find it. Luckily for me, I had several FabFinders along the way, leaving breadcrumbs that helped guide me down my own path.

As I've said before, the journey of *Finding Fabulous* is winding and not always smooth. It can often feel like you take one step forward, only to take two steps backward. I don't think I met anyone who would dispute that! However, it seemed the FabFinders who were really hitting their stride and making the most progress had the strongest and most diverse systems of support. In this chapter, their stories illustrate the power of building support networks with specific intention. Their examples are true testaments to that opening quote: "many wings achieve twice the distance".

In this chapter, I will address the more intangible needs for support that surfaced in my interviews. Regardless of the industry individuals worked in or the type of work they moved toward, some common themes arose: support that encouraged their progress, advocated for their needs, coached their development, brought awareness to their situations, and connected them to other resources and mentors. This isn't to say you won't need support to build your website, do your taxes, or the many other tangible things that will accompany your decisions; it's just that I believe more intangible needs are sometimes the hardest to decipher and most often forgotten.

From the chapter on You, you've learned to ask the important questions and listen to your own heart for answers. The next chapter challenged your beliefs about money and dared you to consider what was possible if you didn't let it hold you back. It's time to fortify those thoughts and decisions by building a group of allegiance around them.

Weaving a Tapestry of Support

I'm no Steven Spielberg, but I don't think you have to be a world-famous movie producer to appreciate how many different roles must be filled to produce a box office hit. Even a layperson like me can imagine the huge number of resources, and the level and degree of support required from each, that must be involved at different stages in order to complete a film. Surely a makeup artist is more important during actual filming than during location scouting. Maybe the actor's agent played a critical role during contract negotiations, but isn't as necessary once the cameras are rolling. What's more difficult for an outsider like me to know is what types of support and expertise are needed, and when to call upon them.

I don't envision that my road to *Finding Fabulous* will lead me to be an Oscar-winning producer, but I do see some parallels between Mr. Spielberg's path and mine. We will both be ten times more successful at achieving our goals if we surround ourselves with the right support at the right time.

After interviewing numerous FabFinders, I've come to appreciate the impact of different types and levels of support, and I've learned that all support is not created equal. I felt the difference in the voice of a woman who told me, "My husband loves me, but he wants me to make money," compared with another who said, "My husband and I trade off the household chores, depending on whose job is most demanding at the time." Progress seemed to vary for those who got coaching from their friends versus those who had hired a professional. And despite the learning and insight some gained from books and online courses, it didn't seem equivalent to those who had attended live events.

My own progress seemed to sputter and spurt according to the various types and level of support I received along the way. A friend's positive words about my blog would encourage me to keep writing, whereas those from a random stranger moved me to make my impact even greater. I learned a lot by reading books and websites about the "experts industry," in which people make a lot of money writing, speaking, and online marketing. However, talking to FabFinders who were actually supporting their families with those activities provided me with a completely new perspective and sense of possibility.

Sometimes I had a lot of people cheering me on, telling me I could accomplish anything. Although that helped me along the way, there were times I wished I'd had a coach to help me figure out how to do it. Other times I'd know what I needed to do, but I lacked the urgency and accountability to do it.

Long before starting the manuscript for this book, I decided to map out my support system. I wanted to figure out when and why I made progress, as opposed to those times when it felt like I was swimming upstream. What was the difference? By that point I had concluded I couldn't do it on my own, but how was my path different from the FabFinders I admired?

I thought I was doing a good job seeking help, yet I was still struggli support in certain areas. Was my network supporting me where I most, and at the level I required to succeed? Was I still trying to do too much on my own?

That's when I started to appreciate the need for a strong tapestry of support. Tapping into my personal struggles and comparing them to the various stories from the FabFinders, a matrix of sorts started to emerge. I like to refer to it as a *tapestry* because I found nine *threads* of support that I believe, when woven together in the right pattern, create a beautiful picture of success.

Nine Threads of a Strong Support Tapestry

Creating the foundation for our tapestry, the interviews revealed three main types of supporters. Even though some sources played more than one role at a time, each one seemed to offer a distinctively different value.

Types of Supporters

- **Cheerleaders**—cheer when you need it most and celebrate your wins.
- **Coaches**—guide, challenge, and help you stretch your capabilities.
- **Accountants**—hold you accountable to your goals and benchmarks.

In addition to the valuable role each of these supporters plays, they also offer a different level of support, depending on their perspective.

Levels of Support

- **At Home**—support you as a person.
- **On the Path**—support your goals in general.
- **In the Arena**—support your specific goals.

Supporters who are "in the arena" can be further categorized according to how much experience and expertise they have in your specific field or industry. This leads to the remaining three threads of our tapestry:

Stages of Support (Supporters who are "in the arena")

- **Similar Stage**—share similar challenges.
- **Further Along**—offer relevant and relatable advice.
- **Ultimate Success**—set the bar high and encourages you to dream big.

To be fair, if I was looking at this list for the first time, I might think, "Holy crap! I need all of that!" Before I lose you in the details of how these things weave together, I want to highlight the fact that most people don't need all of the support categories listed above at any one time. There will be times when stacking one type or another in your favour will keep you on course and moving forward. On the other hand, some types of support could overwhelm you if you aren't ready for them. Think of these threads as a heads-up about what you might need in the future.

This next section will encourage you to think differently about the network of people supporting you. Using examples from the FabFinders, we will discuss each one of the nine threads. As you read through their examples, consider how your current support system could be strengthened by adding sources that play different roles, come from unique perspectives, and have vast stages of experience. Remember, the strength of the tapestry comes from the collective. What could you accomplish if you were able to design the perfect support team?

Types of Support

Imagine a movie star who chooses to rely solely on a film's director to do her makeup and expects the cameraman to help her land a leading role. Instead of working with an acting coach, she asks her fans for advice, and relies on her mom to review her legal contracts. What do you think would happen to her reputation and her career?

Everyone in the above scenario plays a specific role at a specific time. Changing those roles, or expecting someone to play a role he isn't trained for, would result in chaos. What does this have to do with Finding Fabulous? What roles help us along our transformation?

The Cheerleader

When I decided to leave my fifteen-year career in sales and marketing, I didn't need anyone to approve the decision. I didn't have a spouse to answer to or kids to support. I didn't ask my boss's opinion, and I didn't even tell my friends what I was about to do. However, emotionally, I needed my family to support my decision. I needed to know they would be there for me no matter what happened. Not too surprisingly, it came as a bit of a shock to them that I would take such drastic measures, leaving before I had something else lined up.

My sister's initial reaction probably surprised me the most. We've been extremely close since childhood, and to this day I consider her my best friend. I not only wanted and needed her support; I expected it. What I didn't expect was how uncomfortable it would make her. To be fair, I know how much she dislikes change, so her reticence shouldn't have been that shocking. She was uncomfortable *for* me, not *with* me.

Thankfully, after her initial response, it didn't take long for her to become my biggest cheerleader. I know there were many times she didn't understand or relate to what I was going through, but there was never a time when she didn't believe I would figure it out. I can't begin to convey how important that was to my progress. Through my sister's faith, I gained a strong safety net of support—a soft landing for the inevitable stumbles and falls.

Not all the FabFinders were lucky enough to have such a devoted cheerleader to encourage their success. One new entrepreneur who had recently quit her day job and was struggling to grow her healthcare business found a huge source of frustration in her husband's lack of support. Despite providing her some encouragement for the decision to go full-time with her new business, he often made discouraging comments, or threw jabs at her ability to produce a substantial income. Although she possessed many great qualities that assured me she would eventually be very successful, it was obvious that her husband's lack of faith affected her level of confidence. Her own self-doubts seemed to be exacerbated by her husband's fears.

When I consider the three different types of support that came out of the interviews, I'd have to say the role of cheerleader seemed the most fundamental. As trivial as the title may make it sound, I believe it's at the core of making the decision to leap. Before we need coaches who help us achieve what we want or accountants who hold us to it, we need someone to believe in us, even (and especially) when we fail to believe in ourselves. We need to know that if we fail, someone will be there to pick us up and dust us off, and in order to keep going, we need someone to help us celebrate our wins along the way, regardless of how big or small they may seem.

My sister played that role for me. Who does it for you? Who is rooting for you, whether they understand what you are doing or not, and whether you are wildly successful or embarrassingly floundering? If you don't have a tireless cheerleader rooting for you, are you proactively trying to find one?

The Coach

Unlike cheerleaders, when I speak about needing coaches, I'm being quite literal. Just as that movie star can benefit from an acting coach, and athletes like Michael Jordan and Wayne Gretzky needed coaches throughout their careers, so did many FabFinders. Some FabFinders had life coaches to help them clarify what they really wanted; others had business coaches, marketing coaches, and speaking coaches. The more entrepreneurs and small business owners I met, the more I heard about these types of coaches, and it didn't take long for me to realize how critical they can be to accelerating progress. Ironically, I learned that self-exploration is easier if you don't try to do it yourself.

My first coach took me through a process that was not comfortable. She forced me to answer some basic questions, like, "What brings you joy?" As I mentioned earlier, that simple question still brings me to tears when I remember having no answer. The lesson was clear: growth is not comfortable. Unlike the emotional cheerleading I received from my sister, her role was to challenge and make me stretch to be better than I was before. Sure, she also cheered me on, but it was different. In order to encourage me to dig deeper and uncover knowledge, skills, and talents I didn't know I had, she had to go way beyond "you can do it." Her main role was helping me uncover what was already inside of me. Although that may seem like something you can figure out yourself, my experience taught me how much easier and faster it can be with the help of a great coach.

Consider the vast number and types of coaches that exist today. Where could you use some extra guidance? Could hiring a coach make the difference in getting to your goals faster and more easily?

The Accountant

Although at times we might need an actual accountant to manage our finances, in this case I'm not being quite so literal. Perhaps it was my own story more than any other that taught me the importance of accountability. Historically, I had always been really good at getting things done. I'd say I would do something, and then I'd do it. If someone asked me to do something, I'd do it. I assumed that was just my tendency—until I decided to write a book!

The decision to write a book meant I would need to practice writing. After all, I wasn't a writer by trade. I hadn't taken English composition in university, or done any other formal training. At the time, I didn't even write in a journal regularly. I knew I would need to start writing more often if I was going to get better. I had lots of people cheering me on, and I even took an online writing course to get some coaching. After the course ended, I made the commitment to start a blog. I thought I could write a couple of entries a week, every week, to get used to sharing my work publicly. Despite my good intentions to share the FabFinders stories and advice on my new blog, I didn't. Months and months passed by, and interviews piled up on my recording software. What was my problem? Why wasn't I staying accountable to myself?

It wasn't until I decided to take off on a cross-country road trip that I found the accountability I needed. In an effort to appease my family's concern for my well-being and their desire to know where I was, I promised to share my adventures through my blog. Even on the evenings I was too tired to write, I forced myself to stick to that commitment. I knew that the next day I would be on to a new adventure and I'd lose the lesson of the day, but more importantly, I had made a promise to my family. That desire to make good on my promise gave my writing a greater sense of urgency and more meaning than I'd ever had before.

The accountant in your life may or may not be the same person who coaches or cheers you on. In fact, it might not even be a person. For twelve weeks, that online writing course was my accountant. E-mail notifications reminded me of deadlines and set specific guidelines for my learning experience. After that, the promises to my family kept me on track. Regardless of what or who does that for you, the purpose is to hold you strictly accountable to your commitments. Ensuring that you have an accountant not only holds you to your goals, it also reminds you to continually set higher benchmarks for yourself.

Who does that for you? If you don't have anyone, could you proactively create a source of accountability by signing up for a course, hiring someone, or even trading accountability roles with someone else?

The Full Team

What do you think would happen if our fictitious movie producer decided that, instead of cameramen, he would just hire more actors? Or maybe in lieu of a director, he decided to spend the money on better set designers. What a disaster that would cause! I don't think you have to be in the movie business to comprehend the importance of balance in this scenario.

My own experience taught me that having lots of cheerleaders, but no accountants, could make me feel good, but it didn't help me get anywhere. I met others who had great coaches pushing and stretching them, but not enough cheerleaders celebrating their wins and cheering their success along the way.

What is the perfect balance for your team? Do you need coaching to give you direction and guidance? Do you have someone or something to help you accomplish your goals and meet your deadlines? Who cheers you on and helps you celebrate your wins?

Chapter 5: Support

Although many FabFinders had people who played the various roles discussed above, Lisa's story best exemplified how to proactively pull all the pieces together. She called it her "Power Team." I loved the description and how she intentionally set out to surround herself with the right support.

Lisa's Story

Although Lisa's husband had always supported her in many ways, it was a tough sell to get him on board with her latest idea. "He wanted to know when I was going to go out and get a real job, with benefits and a regular paycheck," she says. But Lisa knew she no longer fit the mold of a 9-to-5 corporate job, and that her wellness relied on achieving the freedom associated with being an entrepreneur. Even though her husband didn't fully understand her enthusiasm or her faith in this new idea, she was able to convince him that this time would be different.

After spending years working for other people in the retail industry (managing marketing and promotions for a major shopping center), Lisa decided to go into business for herself. She spent the next fifteen years trying her hand at various entrepreneurial endeavours, including a few direct-selling companies. Recently she teamed up with another woman to form a coaching and consulting firm aimed at helping small local businesses. Unfortunately, the partnership was short-lived, and Lisa was left to build something on her own. Luckily, the experience was long enough to teach her something valuable about the benefit of partnerships.

Not wanting to work completely alone, and recognizing that she needed extra support to be successful, she proactively set out to build what she now calls her "Power Team." As she describes it, a power team is a group of individuals you rely upon to help you grow as a person and as a business owner. Her team currently includes a hypnotherapist who is helping her overcome personal and weight issues that affect her business, along with a life coach who is helping her develop and understand her dreams. "If I can't see the big picture, how am I going to know how to get there?" she asks. Rounding out her team is Jeremy, an accountability partner she met through Toastmasters, a group she initially joined to improve her speaking skills. Signing on with Jeremy as her speaking coach and attending his seminar led to weekly coaching calls. The impact of that regular touch point eventually resulted in their forming a mutually beneficial accountability relationship. Now they work together, refining their business plans, outlining their goals, and holding each other accountable with a weekly (and sometimes daily) call.

A few months ago, Lisa stumbled upon another community of support through a network marketing company that sells self-help and business management books. The more she learned about the material, the more passionate she became about its utility for herself and her clients. It felt like a perfect complement to her coaching business. The books and programs provide another, low-cost option to coaching. The content not only develops her own skills, but also helps clients who are unable to afford her full coaching rates. Additionally, Lisa is able to leverage her skills and experience as a business coach to help others on her network marketing team. That sort of community is already built into the organization and has in essence strengthened her Power Team by providing her with even more cheerleaders and accountability partners.

Exemplifying the benefits of being intentional about the support you receive, Lisa found a way to supplement the emotional support she gets from her husband with the business and personal support she receives from her Power Team. Not stopping there, she was able to add an entire community of support with her network marketing team, thus creating an even stronger tapestry of support.

Impressed and intrigued by Lisa's "Power Team," I immediately set more intention to find myself an accountability partner. It was the first time I started to be more strategic about the people I found to help me. One of the unexpected benefits of doing that was the incredible sense of peace I felt. I hadn't realized how much I was beating myself up for not being able to stick to my intended actions. I finally stopped asking, "What is wrong with me?" Once I shifted that energy to finding the right kind of help, I freed myself up from the shame game I had been playing.

What about you? Are you struggling in any particular area and wondering why? Could balancing out the different types of support you receive free you from your battle?

Levels of Support

If that movie star we mentioned earlier ever did come around to realizing she needed coaching from someone other than her fans, she might have several options. Perhaps she has good friends or family members who could run lines with her and offer tips for improving her memory or timing. Maybe she knows a certified coach who works with performance artists like actors, musicians, and comedians. Although any or all of those individuals might be able to provide some coaching, it isn't hard to imagine how an actual acting coach, especially one who specializes in film, could benefit our movie star.

In addition to the three *types* of support, the FabFinders taught me about the need for varying *levels* of support. The amount of support we need from each of the three types depends on where we are in our progress. The next three threads in our tapestry speak to these levels and highlight how we need them at different points in our journey. In our example, the actress is already a "movie star." Since she is already quite successful, it makes sense to think that she could benefit from coaching with an expert in the film industry. Before she hit it big, coaches with less expertise might have sufficed. It's all about timing and intention. That same movie star might benefit from a family member's coaching skills, helping her manage her finances or learn a new skill.

The same analogy works for the roles of cheerleaders and accountants. As I became more determined to write a book, I needed the encouragement of people who were actual writers. It wasn't enough to have my close friends tell me I could do it. The same went for my need for accountability. Initially, I kept my promises to my family to update my blog, but eventually I had to hire an editor to keep me accountable for finishing this book.

Consider the people who encourage your progress, coach you through your challenges, and hold you accountable. Is the level of support they offer enough for you at this stage? Could you benefit from finding someone with more experience or expertise?

At Home *(primarily supports the person)*

In the interviews, this level of "at home" support surfaced when someone would say, "My husband loves me and wants me to do whatever makes me happy," or when someone might say, "my friends think what I'm doing is really brave."

This form of support comes from individuals in your life who love you, regardless of what you do or whether you succeed or fail. They provide your "soft place to land." For me, my cheerleader was my sister. More than any particular action, she supported me as a person. In terms of a coach, I had a friend who talked me through the decision to leave my job. She couldn't offer me much coaching after I left, but she was integral in helping me take that first leap. I had another friend offer to hold me accountable for writing my blog. She wasn't exactly an expert in blog writing, but that extra touch point added some increased responsibility.

We all need a strong shoulder to cry on now and again, and a familiar face to help us through the rough patches. However, it became clear that this level of support was not always enough. This level of "at home" support is fairly general, and more about supporting you personally rather than specific support for what you are trying to accomplish.

In my example, my sister loves me and believes that I can accomplish whatever I set out to accomplish. She may think I'm a great writer, but how far will that support take me? Although it feels good and does help to build my confidence to a certain degree, my sister isn't a writer. Her early support was essential for me to get started, but once I began to write the book, I needed something more. If a complete stranger who is a published author told me my writing was great, it might provide a different level of encouragement.

On the Path *(support general goals)*

The next level of support comes from people who understand why you are taking the risks and who support your decision. They may not have specific knowledge in your industry or field, but they are further along the path than those "at home."

In the example above, Lisa found someone in her Toastmasters group who could serve as her accountability partner. He wasn't a family member or close friend, but because he was also an entrepreneur, he understood her challenges. He didn't have to be in the same line of work to offer her valuable assistance.

For me, this level of support came from almost everyone I interviewed for my book; their stories taught me that major career shifts can result in major, positive life transformations. They may have worked in different fields, but every single one of them had walked away from a traditional, stable job in a search for something more. Our discussions often turned into mutual coaching sessions as we shared our biggest issues and frustrations, and sometimes we became each other's accountants as we shared updates on our progress.

However, not many of them were writers. They could offer support about things like uncovering my value, starting a business, or optimizing networks, but they couldn't offer much about what it takes to write a best-selling book. I could rely on these people to be cheerleaders, coaches, and even accountants when it came to developing as an entrepreneur, but not so much as an author. For that, I needed something more.

In the Arena *(support specific goals)*

> It is not the critic who counts; not the man who points out how the strong man stumbles, or where the doer of deeds could have done them better. The credit belongs to the man who is actually in the arena, whose face is marred by dust and sweat and blood; who strives valiantly; who errs, who comes short again and again, because there is no effort without error and shortcoming; but who does actually strive to do the deeds; who knows great enthusiasms, the great devotions; who spends himself in a worthy

> *cause; who at the best knows in the end the triumph of high achievement, and who at the worst, if he fails, at least fails while daring greatly, so that his place shall never be with those cold and timid souls who neither know victory nor defeat.*
>
> Theodore Roosevelt

I stole the term for this last level of support from an interview I saw with Brene Brown, author of the best-selling book *Daring Greatly*. Dr. Brown credits the famous speech by Theodore Roosevelt for inspiring her to be in the "arena," daring greatly. Since she has received a lot of feedback, both positive and negative, on her work, she has decided the only comments that matter to her are from people who are "in the arena, also daring greatly."

So let's talk about those people in the arena. The support that can be garnered from other people on a similar path can be extremely valuable to our progress. These people not only understand what and why we are daring to live more fabulously, but they are also in it with us. Their knowledge of resources, depth of experience, and mutual understanding of support needs make these individuals invaluable.

In Lisa's case, her accountability partner was "on the path" in terms of helping with her business, but because he was a speaker and certified speaking coach, and had a lot of experience running speaking boot camps, he was "in the arena" when it came to speaking. Once she decided that speaking would be a part of her business, she hired him as a speaking coach. His knowledge and expertise were at a depth Lisa needed.

For me, I found coaches who were "in the arena" by signing up for a weekend mastermind experience led by four best-selling authors. They provided support about the resources and processes required for publishing, but they also provided guidance for my content because they had written books in my genre. Although—or perhaps because—they didn't know me personally, their expertise provided the support I needed once I had reached the writing stage.

Putting it all together

As we've discussed, the strongest tapestry requires a variety of types and levels of support.

When I decided to quit my job, my friend coached me through the decision. She wasn't an expert or a certified coach, but her assistance helped me through that time. After leaving, I needed a life coach to guide my self-discovery process, and eventually I needed some guidance with my writing process. A writing coach would have been too overwhelming at first, so I went with an online writing course to get started. As I gained clarity about the goal of writing this book, I needed different support. The coaching I received from the best-selling authors was amazing, but I still needed to find an accountability partner. Friends asking if I submitted my weekly blog post were initially a great help, but as I mentioned, it was an editor who finally helped me set firm deadlines and finish this book.

Potentially more important than having a network of support, it's crucial to be clear about what support is needed and when. If my own journey wasn't evidence enough, the FabFinders proved to me over and over again how dynamic those needs are.

Stages of Support

If you have ever watched the Screen Actors Guild Awards or the Oscars, you will appreciate the relevance of the last three threads in our tapestry. Keeping with our movie star example, I want you to consider how actors respond to winning those respective awards. The SAG awards involve actors giving awards to other actors, whereas "The Academy" decides who wins an Oscar. As much attention as the SAG award winners get, it never seems to measure up to the accolades that come with winning an Oscar. The actors themselves seem to be happy with the recognition of their peers, thrilled if those peers are bigger stars then themselves, and overjoyed if it comes from the Academy. Why the difference?

I think it has to do with needing support from people in your field who are at various stages. In the case of movie stars, the "cheerleading" they get from actors at the same level offers a different degree of support than what they might get from those whom they consider at the top of the field. Support from people at the ultimate or highest level—like an Oscar nod from the Academy—is even more distinct.

Remember Michael, our brave magician who stepped onto a stage in front of 250 people without ever having hypnotized anyone? I think he describes this *stage* of support best. When Michael decided to become an entertaining hypnotist, he didn't have a coach or mentor who could teach him the ropes. He didn't have friends in the business, and he didn't feel comfortable telling his family what he wanted. Instead of giving up, he chose to teach himself the necessary skills.

His initial attraction to hypnosis was sparked after watching a performance by one of the biggest names in the business. Excited to learn more, Michael committed to attending any hypnosis show he could find. When he wasn't impressed by the next hypnotist he saw, Michael had the encouragement he needed: even if he never got as good as the first performer, he could definitely be a better entertainer than the second. If that guy was making money with hypnosis, surely he could too! Using the first hypnotist as motivation for his ultimate success, and the second as a more achievable, interim benchmark, he had the key to getting started.

As you consider the support you are getting from people "in the arena" (i.e., in the same field or industry), think about the stage of progress they represent. Could you leverage their expertise, or lack thereof, the way Michael did?

Similar Stage

Someone who is at a stage similar to yours can be a great outlet for discussing your issues and brainstorming solutions. Since they are likely experiencing similar challenges, they understand what you are going through, and might even become your greatest accountability partner.

When I attended the weekend mastermind experience with the best-selling authors, there were ten other first-time authors in the course. It was so nice to have a group of people who understood exactly what I was going through and who happened to be going through it at the same time. We were able to help and support each other as much, albeit in different ways, as the leaders of the course. After the weekend, the leaders put us into two mastermind groups and suggested we continue working together on a frequent basis. They did this because they understood the benefit of having support from others who are at a similar stage.

Further Along

Finding someone who is at a stage you'd like to reach, whether in a few months or years down the road, can give you something attainable to strive for without overwhelming you. These people can be great coaches, since they will often have some best practices and solutions that you can implement right away. They might also be great cheerleaders as they celebrate the smaller wins you achieve along the way.

For Michael, this was the second hypnotist. Before he had any experience with hypnosis himself, he was a bit overwhelmed by the first performer's skill level. Having a middle level to stretch for gave Michael a more attainable goal in the short term. For me, this was working with a FabFinder who was a published writer. He hadn't reached the level of best-selling author yet, but he still had a lot of tips and suggestions that eased my learning curve. Thinking about selling millions of books was exciting but scary! Working with someone who was selling thousands of books felt more attainable and helped me focus on how to accomplish that first.

Ultimate Success

Always aim for Oscar! Looking to people who've achieved the ultimate level of success you would like to attain can inspire you to dream big. Their level of success may be hard to relate to at the current moment, but it can remind you to set your own bar high. They might be the best cheerleaders you can find, since they are encouraging you to keep striving for more while showing you it is possible. As you will learn in the next section, these don't have to be people you know personally.

In Michael's situation, it was the top-performing hypnotist. In mine, it was the leaders of that writing mastermind weekend. In addition, I found authors in the self-help genre and joined their mailing lists to gain more tips and advice. Their encouraging words acted as a sort of cheerleader, while their tips provided some level of coaching experience.

Just as with the other six threads of our support tapestry, each of these threads plays a valuable role when acquired at the right time. Just because someone isn't a superstar yet doesn't mean he can't offer you support. If you are aiming to be a superstar, don't forget to look closer down the road and find someone who is just ahead of you on that same path. Remember that the superstars on that path can also be great supporters. As we'll discuss in the next section, you don't necessarily have to know them, or even meet them in person, to benefit from their help.

Mediums of Support

I hope that by now you've been sold on the importance of a strong, diversely experienced support team. But what if you don't have one? What if, like I did, you start to weave together the loose threads of support you have and realize you are doing way too much on your own? What if you look around and don't see anyone who falls into the categories you know you need? What then?

Remember that Michael didn't have a coach or mentor who could teach him the skills he needed to be an entertaining hypnotist. Instead of giving up, he chose to study the acts of already-successful entertainers in order to teach himself the necessary skills. The other entertaining hypnotists became part of his support network without even knowing it! Now Michael uses those skills to help other hopeful entertainers. He has developed an online course that teaches people the skills he had to learn on his own. His website and courses are a great source of encouragement, coaching, and accountability for anyone unable to find those threads to weave into their own tapestry.

Once you have exhausted the list of your inner circle and recognized you still have unmet support needs, widen your search criteria. Networking groups, MeetUps, business groups, church groups, and other gatherings of like-minded people are great ways to find people in your "arena." If you have trouble finding one, you can always start one of your own and attract others to you. Ideally you will find actual people to interact with who can provide support, but don't negate other options.

Think of Michael's story and contact experts or role models in your field of interest. Even if you can't have one-to-one contact with them, you can sign up for live events with experts, or hire a coach. Live events not only get you closer to the expert you admire, they also typically draw an audience full of people looking for similar levels of support.

Lastly, consider support you get virtually by connecting with role models and experts through books, tapes, podcasts, videos, etc. In Lisa's example, she not only leverages her sales associates as cheerleaders, she also reads the motivational books she sells. Although there wasn't much available at the time Michael was looking to learn, he has now created an online course for anyone who wants to become an entertaining hypnotist.

There are literally thousands of online courses that teach just about anything you could possibly want to do. If you need some guidance or direction but you can't find a coach, try online coaching as a supplement. Think of YouTube as an exhaustive source of cheerleaders, and consider websites like Lynda.com or udemy.com as huge pools of potential teachers and mentors. Sometimes a motivational speech from someone you admire is enough of a cheerleader on a bad day. Or a webinar training session can act as the role of coach when other options aren't feasible. We are more connected globally than we have ever been, and there is no reason you can't use that to your advantage when building your team of allegiance.

Naysayers & Negative Nellies

When I met Natalie, she was struggling. She was struggling to find clients, struggling to make money, and struggling to understand why. Although she was trying all sorts of methods to build her business and she was passionate about her work, she was hitting roadblocks at every turn. It wasn't until she explained her situation at home that I fully understood what was missing.

Her decision to leave her corporate administrative role and pursue a career in personal training seemed even more courageous when she spoke about her family. Her husband was upset with her decreased contribution to the family income, and he constantly gave her grief about attending networking and promotional events for her new business. To add even more stress, her children didn't understand her decision and refused to support what she was doing.

Aside from the fact that she had not supplemented her support network with other sources, Natalie's story was not all that unique. When the FabFinders recounted the early days of their transformations, many of them spoke about the opinions of the people closest to them. Although some had very supportive friends and families, many of them referred to people who thought they were crazy or who tried to talk them out of it. Often, people didn't understand why the FabFinders would risk their seemingly great situations to find something else. Some even hid their decisions from their families until they were well into the transformation. They were afraid of what others would think, and consciously chose to avoid the conversation for fear it would deter their decision or slow their progress.

FabFinders who had the most conviction and were clearest about pursuing their dreams were the least likely to be affected by the naysayers. Even so, inevitably everyone has to deal with people who are opposed to what we are doing, or at least sceptical of our ability to succeed. So what do you do about it? How did the most successful FabFinders handle the skeptics and thrive, despite the pushback?

After all of the interviews and research I've done on the topic, the best advice I can offer is to put it into perspective. Consider the following:

Who are these naysayers?

Are these naysayers in your inner circle? Are they family, close friends, colleagues, people you admire or respect? If they are in your inner circle, I will assume for the sake of argument that they care about you, and you care about them. So why aren't they supporting your decisions? If they are important to you, it may warrant considering what they are saying and why.

Regardless of the reason, you may also have to consider how much time you spend with these people. If it affects your growth and limits your potential, you may have to control the amount of time you expose yourself to their negativity.

For those naysayers who are not in your inner circle, consi[der] [if they] are "in the arena, daring greatly" (as Brene Brown would say[. If they] are "in the arena," their opinion might hold more weight. [These are harder] to ignore than your inner circle, but they might also be worth [more,] depending on how closely related they are to your dreams.

As for everyone else who isn't in your inner circle or "in the arena," ignore them. These are the "armchair quarterbacks," and their view looks pretty good from the "cheap seats," so ignore them.

Why are they sceptical?

Consider the opinions of the people who matter to you. Why are they sceptical? Do they have some information you don't? Are they experts in the field or industry you are working in? If so, ask yourself, "What if they are right?" They don't actually have to *be* right for this question to be valuable. Just reflecting on that possibility will give you a wider perspective and help you determine if you are meant to learn something from their comments or opinions. If you are, take it into account. If not, ignore it.

Alternatively, their comments and concerns could stem from their own self-limiting beliefs. When people are afraid to risk big in their own lives, for their own self-limiting reasons, they fear success in others. Their egos need to be right about this. If you risk big, and start showing success in building the life of your dreams, it threatens their beliefs and poses a blow to their egos. It becomes harder for them to settle for a less than fabulous life when someone has shown that the other side is possible. Whether they are consciously aware of it or not, their egos want you to fail.

These issues have nothing to do with you. It isn't necessary to change their beliefs; just be aware so you can acknowledge them without accepting them as your own truth.

What does your gut tell you?

As a final thought to dealing with naysayers, go with your gut! When it comes down to it, trust that the answers are within you. Your gut instincts are better an anything you will get from someone else, whether it's a supporter or a naysayer. The challenge is in recognizing whether you are listening to your gut or your ego. Sometimes naysayers affect us because they bring to the surface something we're already afraid of.

When I first left the corporate world to discover my passion and purpose, people would often say, "When are you going to get a job and start making money?" Although I had decided to take the time to do some self-growth and explore my options, their comments always really annoyed me. It was my conscious decision not to get a job right away, but their comments unveiled deeper concerns I had about money. I had to come to terms with my own issues before I could really deal with the opinions of others. Once I was secure in my beliefs and the path I was taking, their comments had less effect.

Get very clear about how you feel about your situation so you'll be better prepared to handle naysayers. Remember to consider where they come from, whether they have new information, and whether they are just projecting their own issues onto your situation. Then get back on your path to *Finding Fabulous*!

Roadmap: Build a Team of Allegiance

Now it's your turn. Who will you choose to be part of your crew for the production of your best life?

Do a Needs Inventory

Understanding what support you currently need is the first step to building your tapestry of support. Consider where you are in your progress toward *Finding Fabulous*, building your business, developing yourself, or wherever else you might require support.

Think about Natalie's situation. Natalie might realize that she needs a cheerleader to help her believe she is capable of bringing in the salary her husband expects. She might also decide she needs a business coach to help her achieve that.

What about you? Ask yourself the following questions to get really clear on what you need.

- ☐ What are my biggest barriers?
- ☐ What seems to be holding me back?
- ☐ Where do I wish I had some guidance or positive reinforcement?

The clearer you are about what you need, the easier it will be to build that allegiance around you. If you aren't clear, the process below may help to highlight some of the gaps in your support network.

Take a Support Inventory

Who is currently supporting you? Taking a full inventory of your supporters can heighten your awareness of where some gaps might exist. Think about Lisa's story: she was able to find an accountability partner at a Toastmasters group, and she found a business coach at a networking event.

Consider the following:

- ✓ Friends
- ✓ Family
- ✓ Acquaintances
- ✓ Co-workers and bosses (current or previous)
- ✓ Teachers and professors
- ✓ Mentors and coaches
- ✓ Neighbours
- ✓ Other

Notwithstanding the potential issues mentioned in the previous section about naysayers, your inner circle may be the easiest and quickest way to start building your network. Don't forget to thoroughly contemplate all the people you know. Maybe your cousin's wife has connections or is really task-oriented and could become a great accountant on your team. Or an acquaintance from the gym might become your best cheerleader. Sometimes we overlook the resources right in front of us for fear of rejection or simple lack of awareness. Take the time to look around and appreciate the skills of all the people around you.

Don't forget to capture those individuals who could or would support you if you reached out to them. Remember that your greatest supporters may not always come from those closest to you, or from those who might normally support you in other areas of your life.

Identify the Type, Level, and Stage of Support

Lisa created what she calls her "Power Team." Identifying the various people who supported her (like her husband) and getting clear on how they supported her (personally, not in her business) allowed her to strengthen that team (with others doing similar work). How do the people you listed above support you? Consider the different types (explained earlier in the chapter) as well as the level and stage of support. For each person, mark the type, level, and stage of support they represent for you beside their names on the list.

Types:

- Cheerleader *(provides emotional support and boosts your confidence)*
- Coach *(challenges you to learn and grow)*
- Accountant *(holds you accountable to your goals)*

Levels:

- At home *(people in your inner circle who are supportive of you)*
- On the path *(not in your field/industry, but doing something similar enough to offer support for your general goals)*
- In the arena *(in the same field/industry; supportive of your specific goals)*

Stage:

- Similar Stage *(shares your challenges)*
- Further Along *(offers relevant and relatable advice)*
- Ultimate Stage *(sets the bar high, encourages you to dream big)*

Identify the Gaps / Find a Balance

Map out your support system (from the work you did above) in the ***matrix of support.*** Considering the needs you identified above, do you have enough support in each area? Identify any gaps and consider whether or not lack of support in that particular area is limiting your progress.

	At Home	On the Path	In the Arena *Mark what stage they are at (similar, further along, or ultimate success)
Cheerleaders			
Coaches			
Accountants			

Think about any particular pressures that might be holding you back, and build stronger support to counteract that pressure.

Mix up your mediums

Remember how I was able to use an online course to increase my accountability, Lisa used books to supplement her motivation, and Michael found an expert to emulate. Support systems do not have to rely entirely on individuals with whom you can interact personally. Consider using alternative resources to build your team.

Some examples:

Cheerleaders:

- ✓ Inspirational speakers (live or via podcasts, webinars)
- ✓ Books or audiotapes
- ✓ Stories and biographies of people in your field who have succeeded and the paths they took
- ✓ Self-help books

Coaches:

- ✓ Experts in your field (via online courses, videos, or seminars)
- ✓ How-to books

Accountants:

- ✓ External sources of commitment (depending on your goal) like online courses with assignments, blog/article commitments to another writer, speaking engagements, etc.

Be Proactive

Natalie was struggling in many areas of her business, but she wasn't doing much to build up support. Despite not knowing anyone in the business, Michael went out and found performers who were already successful. No one in my circle of friends was a writer, but I found new friends in a weekend writing course and entrepreneurs in a networking group.

Don't wait for support to show up. Go and find it. If you can't find it, create it. Make a list of resources in your local area that you could tap into, as well as any virtual communities or networks. Start asking around and stay open to the opportunities all around you.

For example:

- ✓ Start a MeetUp group.
- ✓ Start a Mastermind group.
- ✓ Create an online community. Advertise for a coach.
- ✓ Exchange your time coaching or acting as an accountant for someone who will do the same for you.

Manage the Naysayers

Building a positive support system includes having a method of dealing with any naysayers who might be holding you back. Identify the individuals who are hindering your progress and decide whether you will limit your exposure to them.

For those people you do spend time with, put their comments into perspective by considering who the person is and where the comments are coming from.

Reflect on any new information they offer, but don't accept their self-limiting beliefs as your own.

Build an action plan

Using your answers to the above exercises, build a plan to reinforce your support network. Consider how you can obtain extra support for particularly challenging times and create sustainable support for everyday challenges.

Your action plan can include:

- ✓ Clarification of your main issue (e.g., not enough cheerleaders, not enough expertise in my field/industry, etc.)
- ✓ Strategies to overcome that issue (e.g., research more potential supporters, start a new group)
- ✓ Timing (e.g., find an editor by the end of the month, sign up for a course before starting your book)

Reassess

Reassess your needs for support on a regular basis to ensure that your team of allegiance aligns with your current goals and your stage of readiness. If it helps, you can put a recurring appointment in your calendar to remind you to reassess your support network at regular intervals.

Chapter 6: Environment

The first step toward success is taken when you refuse to be a captive of the environment in which you first find yourself.

Mark Caine

"You no have the green thumb," he stated matter-of-factly in his thick Italian accent. The truth of the statement prevented me from being insulted by the strongly opinionated yet well-meaning man I'd hired to clean up the shrubs in my yard. He was right; I don't have a green thumb. I have no idea which plants need more sun and which prefer shade. I don't have a clue as to how much water is too much or too little, never mind which type of soil is better. Gardening is hard!

As I bend over my neglected garden, deciphering which are weeds and which are poorly tended plants, I start to see some parallels with my attempt at *Finding Fabulous*. I begin to wonder if I'm all that different from the floundering plants in my garden, searching for fertile soil in which to thrive. Even though I wasn't born with the natural horticultural gifts of my outspoken gardener, I can understand that a beautiful garden needs an ideal environment. But what exactly does that mean? How am I supposed to know what is ideal and what isn't?

Relying once again on the lessons from the FabFinders, I think back to the first dozen or so interviews I conducted. I remember being surprised to hear that some of them actually used to love what they did for a living. Despite trying to keep an impartial, open mind, I expected to be speaking to people who hated their original jobs. Why the big change? Why would a website designer leave her stable job to start her own company designing websites? Why would a public school teacher walk away from a guaranteed pension so she could teach students through her own tutoring service? What was it about those environments that made them willing to risk what they had in order to do something that seemed so similar?

Although my story is somewhat different from those particular FabFinders, I had to wonder if they could teach me something about the importance of designing the perfect working environment. Was there such a thing? If I could figure out what made up my ideal surroundings, would what I did for a living matter as much? How important was that particular piece in the puzzle of Finding Fabulous?

My own experience taught me the difference between thriving and simply surviving. However, before meeting the FabFinders, I don't think I fully appreciated how much of that was related to my environment. As the industry I worked in evolved, so did the attitudes and ambitions of the people I worked with. As pressures on the bottom line increased, so did the stress of those responsible for it. Understandably, co-workers became more concerned with losing their jobs than doing their jobs. Leadership demanded innovation while tightening the reins on our autonomy. Thinking back to that garden analogy, I'd say it was anything but fertile soil. In fact, it kind of reminds me of a sprout trying to break through concrete.

I'm sure we've all marvelled at that blade of grass or cursed the weed that refuses to be stopped. I guess you could say that's how I felt, like I was constantly pushing through concrete. Although for many years, like that blade of grass, I was "successful," it was anything but easy. I have to wonder what could have happened if I had planted myself in a richer soil.

I got a glimpse of an answer listening to how the FabFinders redesigned their own fertile ground. A former chiropractor found a new mission in sustainable healthcare when she chose not to continue partnering with people who viewed patients as dollar bills. A family therapist found greater joy on stage than she ever experienced in her one-on-one counselling practice. A former teacher found fulfillment in the eyes of her students as she broke through their issues with innovative teaching techniques.

So what is the right environment? Just like the answer for a palm tree is completely different than that for an evergreen tree, I'm quite certain it will be different for you than for me. Though I won't promise this book will give you all the answers you seek, I do think the FabFinders' stories provide a great starting point.

Perhaps, unlike Michael, our entertaining hypnotist, you relish a straight 9-to-5 job, punching a factory time clock. Maybe the certainty of the paycheck or the concrete job expectations give you comfort and reassurance. On the other hand, maybe you are like Chris, and the desire to build something of your own is enticing enough to exchange structured work for more autonomy and flexibility. Perhaps like Tania (the inspirational coach from chapter 3) you need flexibility in where you work so you can travel around the world. Or maybe the idea of being a solo entrepreneur is isolating for you, and you'd prefer to work in a place with lots of other people.

The purpose of this chapter is not to dictate which environment is right or wrong, but to encourage you to get very clear about what is ideal for you. I won't try to convince you that being an entrepreneur is the be-all and end-all, or that a Fortune 100 company is where you will find the most success. I won't assume that you need a collaborative team around you or that working alone is better. I leave that up to you. I will, however, propose that, as the FabFinders taught me, your environment can make or break you. Some environments stifle our ability to tap into our full potential, while others promote and nourish our talents. Some environments spark our creativity, while others blind us to possibilities. In the end, I want you to recognize that finding work you are passionate about isn't enough. I firmly believe that designing the ideal environment in which you do that work is a key step in the journey of *Finding Fabulous*.

The Ideal Environment

> *You can't make positive choices for the rest of your life without an environment that makes those choices easy, natural, and enjoyable.*
>
> Deepak Chopra

Do you know how many factors contribute to creating an ideal environment? One trip to the nursery taught me just how much I didn't know about the ideal gardening environment. How much sun should it have, and at what time of day? What kind of soil should I buy, and how often would it need fertilizing? Do I want perennials, annuals, or some combination of the two? That's way too many factors for me to figure out, at least where my garden is concerned. However, when it comes to my work, and my life in general, I am much more open to doing what it takes. I'm eager to learn every tip I can about creating an environment that will help me thrive.

As the FabFinders shared what was missing from their work situations, I came to appreciate how many factors made up their ideal environments. Highlighting the importance of people, I heard a former data entry clerk compare her progress in an impersonal, large corporation with the family-like atmosphere of a smaller one. Raising the issue of working hours, a business coach recounted how her ideal environment evolved with the birth of her first child; the demands of travel and expectations for working overtime were more oppressive once she had a baby at home. Concerns about compensation played a role in several FabFinders' decisions as they contemplated what they were willing to exchange for the "perks" of their jobs.

In view of everything the FabFinders shared, I came to the conclusion that creating an ideal work environment requires consideration of the following four factors:

- **People** (bosses, co-workers, and customers)
- **Place** (physical space, atmosphere, time of day)

- **Compensation** (financial, recognition, growth opportunities)
- **Expression** (autonomy, creativity, values)

Taking some time to understand how each of these factors contributes to my ideal work environment, I came to appreciate how great an impact the resulting collective could have on my energy levels, my happiness, and my life in general.

People: Whom do you want to work with?

Intuitively, I knew that sun and water are important factors for a healthy garden, even if I didn't know which plants liked what. What I didn't know was how important it is to put certain plants together and keep others apart. Did you know there are male and female versions of some species that need to be side-by-side so they can fertilize each other? And apparently some flowers do better if you plant another low-growing species at their base to shade their roots. Certain varieties are actually poisonous to each other if they're planted in close proximity. It seems that even plants are affected by those around them.

You may wonder why, after confessing that I spent years unfulfilled and unhappy, I stayed at my former company for so long. Why did I wait fifteen years to make a move? The answer is, quite simply, the people. Far and above any other reason, I stayed for the people. Despite what was going on in the organization, or how stressful, frustrating, or even boring my job became, I loved the people I worked with. Luckily, I was fortunate enough to work with some really great, talented, fun, and caring people. Day in and day out, that is really what kept me going.

The FabFinders discussed various types of people they interacted with and who ultimately impacted the creation of their ideal environments.

- **Bosses**
- **Co-Workers**
- **Customers**

ese people affecting you? What kind of boss brings out the best in disposition do you prefer in co-workers? What type of customers do you enjoy serving?

Bosses

"People join organizations; they leave managers." That is a statement I heard when I became a people manager. I'm not entirely sure it was fair to put all that pressure on me as a brand-new manager; nonetheless, it came with two important lessons. The first, which I already knew, was about my ability to impact the experience of my direct reports. I didn't learn the second until I started down this journey of Finding Fabulous. I didn't fully appreciate how important it was for me to help my boss help me. After all, how did I expect my boss to tend to my needs if I wasn't clear about what those needs were?

I like to think that bosses play the role of gardener in our analogy about the perfect environment for plants. Bosses get to decide if we get water, and how much. They decide what "fertilizer" we need to grow, and how often to "prune" our branches when we struggle. In essence, they control a number of different factors that affect our environment. Sometimes they are responsive to the needs of the various species in their garden, and sometimes they aren't. Although plants don't have the luxury of simply leaving a gardener who doesn't meet their needs, we humans do. And we can do it before we wither away.

Conflict with one of my bosses about values and ideals was the initial instigation for my choice to leave my previous job. It was the main reason I felt like I was trying to grow in concrete. I'd walk away from conversations with her wondering if we even spoke the same language. As frustrating as that time was for me, I can now look back on it with a deep appreciation for the lessons I learned. Dissecting the challenges I faced, I realized that it not only kick-started my journey of self-discovery, it also helped me better understand what I need from a leader.

Knowing what you like or don't like about your boss can provide important information about the type of environment you need in order to be successful. As obvious as that may seem, I think we have to dig deep enough to understand

Chapter 6: Environment

what our frustrations might be telling us. For example, if you don't like to be "micro-managed," it could mean you need a lot of autonomy, or that you value a boss who has a lot of trust in you. If you think your boss is unfair, maybe he or she just doesn't understand how you want to be recognized or compensated. Perhaps you respect a leader who comes across as strong and confident, and can't easily appreciate one who radiates a more caring, thoughtful approach. Again, there is no right or wrong answer to any of these questions, only information you can use to set yourself up for success.

You may not always be able to choose your boss. However, you can use a heightened awareness of your needs to communicate better. If you need clarification about what is expected of you, ask. If frequent touch points and too much direction make you feel stifled and micro-managed, speak up. If you need regular recognition to feel valued, share that with your boss. If you find yourself in a thankless job with a manager who is unable to provide any of those things, consider it a clue as to whether you stay or leave. I'm not suggesting you quit your job because of your manager, but I am suggesting that it's a piece of the puzzle in finding an environment that allows you to thrive!

Co-Workers

Creeping Charlie is a form of ground ivy that is more often considered an invasive weed than a plant. Its pretty purple flower belies the fact that this small delicate plant will choke out anything in its path. It is one of those species that you want to be fully aware of so it doesn't destroy your lawn or flowerbeds. Catching it early is the key!

Even though I was lucky enough to be surrounded by amazing people throughout my career, near the end I felt like I was in the "Land of Creeping Charlies." I couldn't understand the motivations or the attitudes of the people around me, and it was suffocating. In that environment, I started to doubt myself, my abilities, and my judgement. I didn't speak up as often, and I felt like my opinion no longer mattered.

As I get really honest with myself, I realize that, although I was suffering in my circumstance, others may have suffered along with me. During my most g situations, I probably wasn't the most fun person to work with. to challenge the status quo was not helpful in a situation where everyone else was just trying to keep their jobs. As much as I could justify my good intentions in the face of the frustrating yet understandable responses of my co-workers, the only truth that matters is that I no longer fit in that environment. By that point, I'm pretty sure I had become the Creeping Charlie.

That's how important it is to surround yourself with the right people; not only will you perform better and feel happier, but so will those around you.

Several of the FabFinders recounted situations which echoed the relevance of this point. A personal trainer told me he struggled with co-workers who saw his degree of ambition as a threat. Although working through those issues taught him valuable lessons about teamwork and people in general, he ultimately found a way to create an environment that was more favourable to his personality and ambitions. A pastor told me how office politics played a huge part in his decision to leave a 25-year postal service career with the government. Despite initially believing his position would allow him to really make a difference, he eventually became disheartened by the actions and behaviours of colleagues he had once respected, and even some who were close friends.

Realizing just how much co-workers affected her overall happiness and desire to go to work, Karen was able to uncover clues to designing her own ideal working environment.

Karen's Story

Years before she became a holistic healer, Karen worked as a data entry clerk for a large corporation. Although I don't think that role was ever meant to spark her true passions, the experience seemed to teach her an important lesson about the type of environment she needed in order to thrive. Struggling to feel at home in the large, impersonal office space, Karen decided to leave for a small, family-owned printing company.

Even though she didn't totally love what she did for a living, she recalls that she loved the people. The difference the atmosphere made was obvious in the tone of her voice as she explained, "The people there were like a second family. I loved that everyone knew each other, and our conversations were casual and more intimate. It felt as if everyone cared about each other." That atmosphere gave her a great environment to work in as she developed other skills and uncovered her true passions.

Even though her path eventually led to entrepreneurship, the early bond she developed with those co-workers solidified her need to work in a caring environment. Maybe it is not too surprising, given how much she values a caring environment, that Karen ended up caring for people as a profession. That insight continues to guide her decisions today as she creates a family-like atmosphere with her business partners and clients.

Depending on how much you interact with your co-workers, how many you have and in what capacity you work with them, can either add to your enjoyment or detract from it. Determining what kind of co-workers you want surrounding you is more about alignment than right or wrong. It takes all kinds of people to make this world go around, but that doesn't mean you have to work with all of them!

Customers

Aside from co-workers and bosses, the other important people who impact your work environment are your customers. When I say customers, I'm referring to both external customers (those who buy your product or service) and internal customers (people who work for the same company and aren't necessarily your co-workers, but require your service). Whether internal or external, these are the people who ultimately judge the quality of your work, and who might even determine if you have a job in the future. Even more importantly, I think customers have the ability to impact our energy, attitude, and even our efforts.

Do you like serving the people you serve? Do you feel grateful to be able to help them in whatever way you can?

My interview with Shannon brought the importance of the customer to the forefront. As a website designer for a large firm, Shannon was required to work on projects for several different companies of varying sizes, in various industries. Listening to her describe her feelings about working for some of those customers was enlightening. I could sense how conflicted she was. In particular, the strong values and sense of responsibility she has for the environment made it difficult for her to work for certain customers: how could she design a website to help increase business for a company she believed was harming the environment?

It was a great point, and one that eventually led her to leave and start her own firm. One of the overarching goals for that new company was to select clients who fit her value system—ones who were contributing positively to her community. I have to imagine that the energy, effort, and passion that went into her work for those clients were second to none.

Depending on how much of your day-to-day activities are spent interacting with your customers, this factor may or may not be important to your overall ideal environment. For example, a retail salesperson spends the majority of his time working with customers, whereas a car mechanic might spend only a fraction of the time with his. The mechanic may not love talking to customers, but since he spends most of his time hidden underneath their cars, it may not be as big an issue for him as it is for the salesperson.

Whether we're conscious of it or not, I feel we work harder for things and people we believe in. Consider some of the clients you really like or respect. What do your efforts look like for them, versus others you may merely tolerate out of obligation? I believe that if we can choose the customers we get to serve, at least to some extent, we will give a more authentic effort, and we'll be more fabulous as a result.

Places: Where do you work?

> *I always wanted to be a teacher,*
> *I just ended up teaching in the world's*
> *largest classroom.*
>
> **Oprah Winfrey**

When I met the FabFinders, the concept of designing the ideal physical workspace took on a completely different meaning. I guess I had been looking at it purely from a logistical perspective. I thought about whether I liked working in a big, busy office or if it was more ideal to work out of my home. I debated what kind of hours I'd rather work, and thought about the type of people I wanted surrounding me. What I never fully appreciated was how much tweaking those components could result in a completely new career. I didn't realize how much I had been limiting my possibilities by assuming certain jobs had to be done a certain way in a particular environment. After all, does a teacher have to teach in a classroom? Does a district judge have to lead from behind a bench? Does an engineer have to use her problem-solving skills for a particular type of problem?

The environment as it relates to a physical workplace has never been as fluid as it is today. Now more than ever, the digital world in which we live allows people to work remotely, virtually, and with more mobility. People are able to create jobs for themselves that didn't exist a few short years ago. Think about virtual office assistants, YouTube celebrities, and professional bloggers as evidence of the possibilities. After hearing so many examples of how FabFinders created their own unique environments and how they are thriving in them, I now firmly believe it is an essential component to *Finding Fabulous*.

Julia's story is a great example of what can happen when you don't let your physical surroundings dictate your choices.

Julia's Story

> *Sometimes the physical surroundings of an environment can blind someone to other possibilities. "I thought I had to be a counsellor because that was what I was trained to do," explains Julia. A master's*

degree in counselling, combined with a natural empathetic disposition, seemed to make her the perfect counsellor. Nearly a decade at a community mental health centre gave her the opportunity to help a lot of children, families, and individuals. Despite feeling some gratification at being able to help others, there was an underlying unhappiness she couldn't seem to shake.

One day she snapped at her family for laughing out loud at a television show. A few days later, her ten-year-old son was consoling her after a particularly hard day when she realized, "Nothing happened to me!" When had she started to take on the issues and emotions of her clients? When had her unhappiness begun to affect her family?

As her awareness grew, she realized her job didn't allow her to be who she really was. An avid follower of spiritual leaders like Marianne Williamson, Deepak Chopra, and Wayne Dyer, Julia believes in the power of positive energy and affirming messages; her job was the exact opposite. At home, she wouldn't even watch the news because of its concentration on negative information. At work, she was trapped inside a room with patients who recounted sad, depressing stories all day long. She wasn't living the very principles she was trying to convey to her clients. In addition, she lived in a small town, and the private nature of her work didn't allow her to acknowledge her clients outside the clinic. This made for a very isolating environment.

Julia had always been naturally outgoing, and she loves to laugh and socialize—things she couldn't do as a private counsellor. Thinking back to her earlier years as a party planner, she could remember some of the things she loved about that job. Although it was much more fun and social, at the time she longed to have the ability to help more people. It wasn't until Julia stumbled upon the experts industry that she discovered she could combine the best of both worlds: she could still be a counsellor of sorts, while changing the environment in which she did it.

Chapter 6: Environment

Leveraging a decade of experience working with her clients' pc along with the personal experience gained from raising he two children, Julia decided to share her expertise in handling parenting issues. Speaking, running seminars, writing, and coaching allow her to counsel parents on what she believes is the most important job they will ever do. Her environment has changed drastically, from the ability to add humour into everything she does to the physical space she does it in. The stage allows her to express herself fully as she entertains and educates parents, while her website and blog allow her to connect with an even greater number of people.

Reflecting on her transformation, Julia offers this advice to others who are stuck in less than ideal environments: "Open yourself up to seeing possibilities by focusing on what makes you feel more you. Doing the things that make you happy will also make others happy." Her success is a great example of how changing your environment can help you take the step from surviving to thriving.

Despite being inspired by Julia's story, I have to admit that I still struggled to understand what it could mean for me. I knew that my skills as a sales rep, people manager, and marketer were transferrable, but I didn't immediately know what I wanted to do with them. It took some work to grasp which components made up my ideal environment. I had to consider things like the physical space. Did I want to work in an office full of people, in the outdoors surrounded by nature, or some combination of the two? I thought about the atmosphere my surroundings would create. Did I want a serious, formal environment, or somewhere people could laugh, get silly, and be free to express themselves? And I thought about the timing of my workday. I'm a morning person, and my energy tends to lag in the mid-afternoon hours. Could I design a career around my desired time of day? Taking these individual pieces—shifting them around and pulling them back together—helped me start to form a new picture of possibility for my future and gave me new inspiration.

In an effort to formulate the ideal physical environment, the FabFinders considered:

- **Physical Space** (building, location, etc.)
- **Atmosphere** (tone, mood, and ambiance)
- **Working Hours** (how many and what time of day)

Taking time to reflect on each of these components can give us more clues to the environments in which we thrive, and can help us paint a clearer picture of what we really want.

Physical Space

Have you seen the movie *The Internship*, with Vince Vaughn and Owen Wilson? It was filmed at Googleplex, in San Jose, California and offers a great depiction of a non-traditional workspace. I'm sure there are others, but it is perhaps one of the best examples I've seen of a large corporation that's attuned to the impact of its physical workplace. Maybe you've seen pictures of the infamous slides in their main lobbies, or heard about the different play zones set up around their offices. In addition to looking really cool, Google's physical environment sends a very specific message to its employees, and it sets a specific tone. If you need solid walls and complete silence to work, you might be distracted by the rubber balls used as chairs, open concept spaces, and sand volleyball courts in the parking lot, but I'm guessing that Google believes this particular environment sparks creativity and innovation. They are optimizing their physical surroundings and intentionally setting the tone to attract a specific type of employee.

The company I worked for was quite the opposite. The head office was extremely formal, with lots of closed offices and big boardrooms filled with flip charts and LCD projectors. As nicely decorated as those offices were, the physical layout was set up for PowerPoint presentations, data analysis, and structured agendas. It amazes me to think how differently I view that space today compared to fifteen years ago. I remember the first time I stepped into the multi building complex. I was in my mid-twenties and at an early stage in my career. Those walls felt like opportunity to me. The sheer size and number of offices told me there was room for growth and advancement—the archetypical career ladder laid out in front me. Now I see nothing but a box. Convention. Confinement. I see all the things I don't want.

Although a lot of things have changed there over the past couple of decades, perhaps none have changed as drastically as I have. *I've* changed. I no longer want the big corner office or all it implies. I don't need the golden nameplate with some impressive title plastered to my door. I've learned that my creative soul wants an environment to match, and my energy is much better suited to more dynamic surroundings with fewer rules and processes. Even as I write this book, I'm figuring out what surroundings inspire me most. I move from room to room in my house before conceding the need to find a quaint little café. I toggle between my laptop and the sticky notes plastered to a blank wall in my dining room. Eventually I uproot my entire life, leaving wintery Canada behind as I search for sun and inspiration in California. As I write this, I'm soaking up that sun, poolside! It makes a difference. I feel my energy and my creativity ebb and flow as my environment changes, and it reminds me to stay aware so I can adapt as necessary.

What do you sense in your physical space? Do the walls around you, or the lack of any, engage your highest self and allow you to tap into your genius talents?

Atmosphere

Through a lot of introspection, Julia realized she loved to be on a stage, speaking in front of hundreds of people. Being cooped up in an office all day didn't align with how she wanted to spend her time. More importantly, she knew she loved to laugh and have fun. It was more than just the physical space; it was the tone, the mood, and the energy in that space. She longed for an atmosphere that was less sombre and depressing than what she found in her one-on-one counselling practice. Although she was grateful for being able to help those people, she longed for the energy and interaction that comes with helping hundreds of people from a stage. The key to creating her ideal environment was to go beyond what she knew about counselling jobs and focus on how she could help people in a completely new atmosphere.

Just prior to leaving my corporation, major renovations were made to the head office. The idea was to replace all the closed office spaces with cubicle groupings that would allow for more collaboration and informal brainstorming. Although the idea sounded admirable at the time, I think they missed the mark. Remember, this was a company that spent decades boxing people in. The company was full of individuals who were used to having four walls and a door they could close. Walking down the hallways of the new "collaborative" spaces, you could almost hear a pin drop. It was as if people were afraid to speak above a whisper.

At the time, I worked remotely from home, and I would get the "hairy eyeball" from colleagues any time I would visit. I have this loud, booming voice that just didn't fit with their idea of appropriate. Wasn't the point of taking down all the walls to make a place where people would actually talk? Why was it frowned upon when someone actually did?

The way I felt during those office visits provided me with more clues to the kind of atmosphere I wanted to work in. I wanted it to be okay to laugh at work. I wanted spontaneous brainstorming sessions to get loud and exciting. I didn't want everything to be so serious all the time!

How about you? Does the atmosphere of your workplace fit your personality? Does it bring out the best in you?

Working Hours

They say timing is everything. Even that ideal garden I've been trying to build is affected by time. Not only do some flowers need more sun than others, apparently morning sun is different from evening sun. The length of time the sun is on each side of the garden will also change the environment, as well as the amount of nutrients and water the plants require. Timing is everything.

I don't know where you grew up, but I'm willing to bet that a huge percentage of people you knew worked 9-to-5, forty hours a week. I grew up thinking that was when people worked if they had an *ideal* job. It was better than working only part-time, since you made more money, and it offered a better lifestyle than shift work. Those were the options. But the times, they are a-changin'!

With best-selling books like Tim Ferriss' *The 4 Hour Work Week*, there seems to be a trend toward people shifting the paradigm that requires working forty to sixty hours a week in order to make a great living. In his book, Ferriss talks about the "new rich" and presents the idea that a new generation of workers considers not only the amount of money they earn, but also the amount of hours they have to put in to earn it. It seems *time* is the new currency. The length of time his book remained on the New York Times best-selling list should be evidence enough that people are eager to figure this out.

The FabFinders confirmed this for me as they spoke about longing for more freedom with their time. The law clerk I met wanted to be able to play golf more often with her fiancé. The lawyer-turned-motivational speaker didn't want her life chewed up by sixty-hour workweeks. A teacher-turned-business coach wanted the hours she worked to coordinate with the school day so she could spend more time with her kids.

Although more businesses are adopting this idea of a flexible workday, the more common examples I came across were from a new brand of entrepreneurs. Those entrepreneurs that built businesses off their expertise or coaching skills seemed to have the most flexibility with regard to where and when they worked. Angela, the former pharmaceutical sales rep, balanced her time between selling a new product, coaching physicians, and training corporations. She had full control of her time because all three of those businesses were her own. Their diversity allowed her to dial up one or the other, depending on whether she wanted to take off on vacation or simply didn't want to work on Mondays or Fridays. Mikey, the former HR director and father of four, scheduled time for entertainment gigs and training around his family's schedule, allowing greater flexibility than his corporate job. At the same time, publishing his first book added some passive income, so he was able to work fewer hours while earning the same income.

The more life and business coaches I met, the more I understood how important timing is to creating an ideal life. Several of them got to a place in their businesses where their incomes were capped by the amount of hours they were able to work. One-on-one coaching tied them to a schedule nearly as much as a corporate job. The flexibility was greater, but not the ability to work fewer hours. Those who wanted to work Ferriss' idea of a four-hour workweek needed to assess what they were willing to do to make that happen.

Creating a passive income source is a solution, but it is anything but passive in the beginning. I've heard Tim Ferriss regret his choice of that title, and he finds himself constantly clarifying what it means. Nonetheless, this concept of creating a passive income stream is becoming more popular, and people are getting more creative at how they accomplish it. A consultant-turned-photographer used real estate investments to supplement her business income, while Lisa augmented her hourly coaching business with sales from network marketing. Michael, our entertaining hypnotist, used his knowledge to create an online course he could sell to others wishing to learn the skill. The course not only helps individuals around the world, it also provides an ongoing income source for Michael, even while he sleeps!

In my case, I'm not stuck on the number of hours I want to work in a day. Flexibility is much more important to me. Passive income sounds good because I like to work hard when I'm working, and play hard when I'm playing. I would love to find a way to work really hard to create something that will eventually keep working for me while I'm playing. Ideally, the work will feel like play, but until that happens I still want a flexible schedule. I want to be able to take off on vacation several times a year, or even at the drop of a hat. I don't want to be tied to anyone else's schedule or their idea of appropriate working hours.

How about you? What is your ideal work schedule? Is there a particular time of day you prefer to work? How many hours per week are you willing to put in to build the life of your dreams?

Compensation: How do you like to be recognized?

If you pick the right people, give them the opportunity to spread their wings and put compensation as a carrier behind it, you almost don't have to manage them.

Jack Welch

When I was a teenager, I worked at McDonald's. At the time, it was a really great job. They gave me free uniforms, half-priced food, and flexible hours that allowed me to work around my school schedule. There were monthly crew events, summer BBQs, and an elaborate Christmas party as added incentives. I think I started out making a whopping $3.25 per hour! Initially, that amount was enough to compensate for the long hours I spent standing at the drive-thru window and the number of ornery customers and screaming children I had to deal with. It gave me a little spending money for the weekends, and even allowed me to save enough for a school trip to France. All in all it was worth it—until it wasn't.

Living in an auto-industry town, I saw many of my friends get jobs working the lines at Chrysler and GM. They worked part-time on Saturdays and Sundays, and with overtime pay, they earned about five to ten times more than I made all week. They didn't work any harder than I did; they weren't required to have any more education or special skills, yet their pay was substantially more. All of a sudden my paycheck didn't seem quite worth it.

Although the actual compensation for the work I was doing hadn't changed, my perception of its worth did. Once that switch was made, it became very difficult to do my job. As much as I tried not to let it affect my performance, I became resentful and even bitter doing a job I actually used to like. I started to detest the smell of fried food on my clothes and the way the polyester shirt felt on my skin. I loathed dealing with the drunk teenagers who frequented the drive-thru at three a.m. and the crying two-year-olds who had just been told we were out of their favourite treat-of-the-week. It was perhaps my first lesson in Finding Fabulous: compensation is relative.

Despite having learned that lesson at fifteen, it has taken me a little longer to understand just how much compensation plays into my overall happiness.

Although we spent some time in the Money chapter figuring out what money is worth to us, we didn't address this overall idea of compensation. After all, financial incentives are only one way to be remunerated for our work. How important money is, compared to other forms of compensation, might vary depending on your financial situation, what stage you're at in your career, or any other number of factors. As the FabFinders described their transformations, it was clear that their priorities for different types of compensation had evolved along the way.

The three main types of compensation identified by the FabFinders were:

- **Financial** (cash, gifts, stocks, medical benefits, pensions, etc.)
- **Recognition** (verbal, titles/roles, awards)
- **Growth & Development** (opportunities for learning and developing)

Only you can decide what you are worth and how you want to be compensated for the value you offer. Regardless of whether your idea of compensation is "realistic" or not, it pays to be aware of whether it is aligned with your work or not.

Financial

> *I act for free, but I demand a huge salary as compensation for all the annoyance of being a public personality. In that sense, I earn every dime I make.*
>
> Michelle Pfeiffer

Shortly after leaving my corporate job, I learned just how much money could affect my sense of self-worth. I have never really been driven by money, so it came as a bit of a shock that it affected my overall happiness.

Chapter 6: Environment

Not really knowing what I wanted to do, I agreed to do some part-time marketing consulting for a small local business. Initially, the financial compensation didn't really matter to me, so I naively agreed to work for a low hourly wage. I mistakenly thought it didn't matter what they paid me, because I didn't need the money. However, as time passed and I learned that similar consultants were making three times more than I was, it started to bother me.

Why wasn't I worth that much? Didn't I have just as much experience and talent as those others?

More importantly, I realized that the lower rate affected the type of work the company assigned to me. They would ask me to do work that wasn't really my area of expertise because it was cheaper than having someone else do it. They didn't respect the expertise I brought to the table, and weren't giving me the opportunity to show what I could really do. How did that happen? Why weren't they taking me seriously? With more experience, and as I clarified what I did and didn't want, I realized it was my fault. I set myself up to be undervalued because I hadn't decided what value I offered. Whether we like it or not, people place more value on things they pay more money for, including the people who work for them.

That experience taught me two valuable lessons. First, despite not being motivated by money, it can still make me feel undervalued when I'm paid less than what I'm worth. That feeling can spill over into other areas of my life and affect my overall self-confidence. Secondly, I learned that I don't like exchanging my time for money. I prefer to be compensated for the value of what I create, rather than an hourly rate. If I came up with an amazing marketing slogan in ten minutes, how would I charge for that? Is that only worth one-sixth of an hourly rate? Regardless of whether something takes me two minutes or two days, I want compensation for the value, not the time. Both of those lessons provide important direction when it comes to designing my ideal environment.

At a conference I attended shortly after leaving my corporate job, I heard Brendon Burchard explain this idea of relativity in financial compensation. He explained how he came to charge so much for his one-on-one coaching sessions. Apparently, as he figured out which parts of his business he enjoyed doing most—like running seminars, writing books, and online marketing—

he realized he didn't want to spend as much time doing individual coaching sessions. Since coaching was less enticing to him, he decided to raise his price to a point he figured most people wouldn't pay. Surprisingly, some people were willing to pay the higher amount. I think it was something like a thousand dollars an hour, then five thousand, then ten thousand. As time went on, and he had even less time and interest in that area of his business, he figured out an amount of compensation that made it worthwhile for him. I think he gets paid something like fifty thousand dollars an hour now for an individual session!

What financial compensation is right for you? What is your time worth? How much money would you want in order to do your dream job? As with most things we are discussing in this book, not everyone will have the same idea about what financial compensation is right for them. Luckily, there is no right or wrong answer, just the answer that helps you create your ideal situation.

Another FabFinder told me that he loved what he did so much that he was willing to perform for free. He said the reason he charges five figures per hour is to compensate him for the parts of the job he doesn't enjoy, like getting up at the crack of dawn to catch a flight or waiting around in a hotel room before he goes on stage.

This is something to keep in mind. Since we are on a path to Finding Fabulous, many of us will find work that we'd be willing to do for free. That doesn't mean you have to do it for free.

Figure out your value, consider what other parts of your job you want to be compensated for, and then ask for what you are worth.

Recognition

Although recognition is often packaged as financial rewards like cash or stock options, it also comes in a variety of other forms. From a simple thank-you, to a leadership title, or even a prestigious award, there are many ways a person can feel recognized.

As a former people manager, I know very well how challenging it can be to align the type of recognition with its recipient. Some sales representatives on my team wanted to be acknowledged for their successes in front of their colleagues, while others cared more about the money award that came with it.

In that role, I came to appreciate how important recognition is, regardless of what form it takes. For years, our normal assessment procedure involved taking each employee through an annual performance appraisal, giving him or her a grade and accompanying salary increase. One particular year, though, the company decided to change the rating system. The highest achievable score would still be six points, but we were asked to give nearly everyone a three. So we had a six-point scale where six was impossible, five was nearly impossible, and four was awarded to only a select few. Basically, they made us scale everyone's scores back by a point compared to previous years. Why? What did that accomplish, other than making people feel bad about their progress? For the life of me, I couldn't figure out what purpose that served.

That experience left its mark and taught me something valuable about recognition. Even though most of my team received salary increases that were similar to the previous year, the lower scores impacted their morale. The money didn't make up for the lack of feeling recognized for how hard they were working. How were they supposed to work harder for a company that didn't recognize the work they were already doing?

Not everyone needs a ticker tape parade every time they accomplish something. If you are someone who does, great, go where the parades are! If not, consider what you do need as recognition. Essentially, everyone wants to matter. Does your environment give you the type, level, and frequency of recognition you require? If not, what's missing?

Growth & Development

Have you ever gone to a nursery to pick out trees, shrubs, or flowers for your garden? It never ceases to amaze me how bright, strong, and healthy everything looks. I can never get my hanging baskets to look that colourful or grow that full. How do they do it? I mean, besides having experienced gardeners tending the plants 24/7, is there another trick? I asked this question of one of my friends who happens to be an amazing gardener, and she told me their secret. It's the fertilizer. Apparently, they don't just water the plants on a regular basis; they add fertilizer to help stimulate their growth.

I started to think about how similar that was to my efforts at finding the ideal environment. Maybe finding the right location, surrounding myself with the right people, and ensuring I was financially well-compensated weren't enough. What if I had a little "fertilizer" to ensure I grew strong and healthy in the process? What would that look like in the garden of my best life?

When I think about this topic, I'm taken back to all the interviews I've done with the FabFinders who worked in network marketing. I think about Jess, the law clerk, who developed the confidence to present in front of people. She was learning so much about starting her own business while developing the interpersonal skills she needed to be successful. Then there was Lisa, the business coach who was using the books and CDs from her network marketing company to train small business owners and develop her team-building skills. I heard a family member tell me how much she grew every time she attended a national conference and heard success stories from her colleagues. Regardless of what type of product the various companies sold, they seemed to all have one thing in common: a strong focus on developing their people.

The more people I spoke to who were in this line of work, the more I came to appreciate how the companies positioned this part of their offering. Whether it was through print and audio materials, one-on-one mentoring, or large national conferences, it was clear that training and development were positioned as critical success factors. It seemed (at least to this outsider) that individuals were inspired toward continual learning with all kinds of options and resources. Watching the FabFinders light up as they described the available opportunities had me thinking that this was one of the most valuable things this kind of environment offered.

By contrast, I think about how this was approached in my previous company. When I was a people manager, we had a system called IDP, or Independent Development Plan. I can't tell you the number of conversations we had as a management team about how to utilize this resource with our teams. We debated about whether the individual needed to initiate and manage his or her own IDP, or whether the manager should insist that everyone have an IDP. I remember the first few meetings I had with individuals on my team about their development plans. The conversations went something like, "Well, my last manager wanted me to …" or "I was supposed to complete …" It sounded more like a punishment than an opportunity for growth. Why was that? Wasn't my company offering something similar to the network marketing companies? Why wasn't it accepted as readily?

Perhaps the need for this type of environment is as unique as each individual. Take my old team, for example. Some individuals didn't want a development plan. They were happy doing their jobs, and didn't seem to need or want any additional "work" to do. Some were anxious to move up the corporate ladder, and were willing to do anything I suggested that might get them closer to that goal. For others, growth was important to them, but they either lacked the awareness of what they wanted, or were so overwhelmed with daily work tasks that they didn't have the capacity for anything more. Maybe the biggest mistake we were making as a company was assuming this was an important component for every employee.

How about you? Do you want to be in an environment where you have the opportunity to grow and develop? Do you want that to be formalized and guided by your company, or would you prefer it be more flexible and self-guided? As you can probably guess by now, there are no right or wrong answers, just more clues in designing that ideal environment for your growth.

Expression: Do you get to be you?

An orange tree will always be an orange tree. Plant that tree amongst a field of apple trees, and it will still produce oranges. The only problem: apple trees and orange trees require different environments. That orange tree is going to struggle to be the best it can be if you force it to live in an environment made for apples. I believe people are the same.

There is a difference between not understanding who you truly are and not being able to express yourself because of your environment. Some environments might lend themselves more to helping you figure out who you are; others might limit your expression of it. The FabFinders taught me several ways in which an environment can limit self-expression. Tanya's story about leaving mainstream radio to create a *Good News Only* program was a great example of the importance of autonomy. Shannon's story about being reprimanded for speaking up about an issue on one of her projects highlighted the need for the expression of quality.

Overall, the FabFinders taught me various areas where our environment can impact our ability to express ourselves:

- **Expressing our Autonomy**
- **Creative Expression**
- **Expression of our Values**

Expressing our Autonomy

Karrie helped me understand the importance of autonomy and how the pursuit of it can result in doing a traditional job in a completely new way. Similar to Julia's story, she demonstrates just how important it is to create an environment that allows you to be *you*. Not only do I think her new environment is more beneficial for her, I also believe she is able to offer much more to others as a result.

Karrie's Story

> *Listening to Karrie describe her previous working environment as a sort of second home, I start to wonder what would ever make her leave. After all, a teacher's salary and the security of the pension that goes along with it aren't things you easily walk away from. So why did she, after twenty-two years?*
>
> *Although her mother recalls that Karrie always wanted to be a teacher growing up, she wavered during university, trying her hand at chartered accounting and clinical psychology before landing herself in teacher's college. Perhaps those early experiences affected her enough to give her a perspective that was different from most of her colleagues.*

"*I always felt like a square peg in a round hole,*" *she admits. The rules and regulations that accompanied structured federal education were often challenging for Karrie; she struggled to understand various initiatives and why they were being implemented. The environment didn't provide her with enough flexibility or autonomy to express her creativity as an educator. She adds, "Sometimes I don't like to play by other people's rules, especially if I don't think it is in the best interest of the children."*

More than two decades of frustration and feeling hemmed in hadn't been enough to inspire Karrie to change. She envisioned herself coasting along nicely until retirement, when she would have the freedom to do what she wanted. Then one day, her eyes were opened to new possibilities when her teaching partner of twelve years made the bold choice to retire early and explore artistic endeavours. Seeing how much her previous partner blossomed as a result of that decision was the push she needed.

All of a sudden, the tutoring she enjoyed doing during summer breaks seemed more like a new opportunity rather than a mere hobby. The emotion in her voice was evidence of her passion as she recalled, "A parent was thanking me profusely when her son, who had struggled for many years prior to working with me, graduated high school with honours." Feeling like she could make a bigger difference by working with individual students and tailoring her teaching to their needs, she decided to open her own tutoring company. Finally, she would be able to leverage some of the business skills she learned in university while stretching her creative muscles by finding new ways to break through to struggling students.

Focusing on the value she can offer each student has been her best strategy. As she started to release her anxieties about making enough money, the clients she needed to make her business successful appeared. "It was kind of like magic," she says with a laugh. Summarizing the main reason for starting her new business, Karrie reveals her definition of success. For her, it is all about having the freedom to set and pursue her own goals while being able to support and spend time with her family.

Karrie demonstrates what is possible for someone who already loves what she does for a living, yet still dares to go on a quest to Find Fabulous. Leveraging skills she already had, tapping into a friend's experience for inspiration, and being brave enough to try something new, she found a way to express her autonomy and her creativity. As for the outcome, it is easy to see how the children she teaches, as well as Karrie herself, are thriving in this newly created, fabulously customized environment.

What could you accomplish if you dared to express more autonomy?

Creative Expression

Long before I recognized my own creativity, I longed for it. I might not have known what it was, but I still longed for it. As a marketing manager, it would pain me when I had to hand over a project to our "creative agency." Any time my idea to add a little fun and uniqueness to a project were kyboshed by our legal department, it frustrated me. Whenever my ability to respond to a customer's need was prevented by industry regulations, it annoyed me. I needed more creative freedom! I hated doing things "the way they've always been done." Being creative was something that excited me and brought me joy. That should have been enough of a clue that working in a strictly regulated industry was not the environment for me.

FabFinders like Maria and Twila spoke about this type of expression as they struggled to find their fabulous environments. Remember how, despite choosing to enter the field of engineering, Maria was drawn to courses that allowed her to express her natural creativity; eventually her need to express that creativity surfaced when clients recognized her ability to do creative as well as technical designs. Twila's ability to express herself was only temporarily halted when she chose to leave the music industry for real estate. Eventually her need for a creative outlet led her to create a company that gave her that space. Years later, she naturally gravitated to an entrepreneurial environment that allowed her to express her need to connect with people on a deeper level.

What environment allows you to fully express your creative side? Does your current environment help or hinder your ability to express yourself creatively?

Expressing our Values

On the road to *Finding Fabulous*, understanding what you value can provide critical information about who you are and what you want. The former postal service employee remembered always having a calling to be a pastor, but it wasn't until he felt his values weren't aligned with his environment that he finally chose to answer it. You already read how a website designer's values about the Earth's environment affected the type of customer she wanted to serve. And we discussed how a radio producer's values forced her to give up mainstream radio in an effort to spread positive news stories. Clarifying your values can help you design an environment to thrive in, while aligning with people, products, or services that match your values can set you up for success.

Jessica thought her passion for hot tubs and their therapeutic benefits made selling them the perfect environment for her. "Some of the best conversations I had with my dad happened in the hot tub," she tells me. It was easy for her to sell that lifestyle to customers because she believed in it so strongly. What she didn't believe in were the sales tactics of the storeowner. After learning more about the water systems and studying water chemistry analysis, Jessica realized they were selling a $1600 salt system that didn't work. Not feeling comfortable lying to customers, she tried to sell her boss on a different solution. Unfortunately, he made a lot of money from the systems and refused to listen. When that same boss reneged on his promises to give her benefits and short-changed her a commission check, the writing was on the wall: this was not a healthy environment for her to stay in.

With her new expertise in water chemistry, Jessica decided she could open her own business. When I asked her what she believed her purpose was, Jessica told me she thinks our greater purpose in life is to help others in whatever form we can. For the immediate future, Jessica is opening a mobile water testing company and selling chemicals online. She hopes to build a platform to offer lessons that help people understand how to manage the water in their hot tubs, and she also plans to sell other all-natural home solutions. In addition to meeting her purpose of helping others, being an entrepreneur allows Jessica to fully express the values she believes in every day.

Overall, the FabFinders taught me about the importance of being able to express myself in many ways. I learned that I want to be able to express my creativity in an autonomous way that allows me to deliver the highest quality of work I can, and I don't want to compromise any of my values in the process.

Which values are most important to you? Does your environment allow you to express who you truly are?

Roadmap: Design An Environment to Thrive In

Now it's your turn. Which elements of your environment are limiting your progress or preventing you from reaching your dreams?

- **People** (bosses, co-workers, and customers)
- **Place** (physical space, atmosphere, time of day)
- **Compensation** (financial, recognition, growth opportunities)
- **Expression** (autonomy, creativity, values)

Ask yourself the following questions to gain a better understanding of your current environment, or answer them with an eye toward your ideal environment.

People

What kind of people do you want in your environment?

Remember how supported Karen (the holistic healer) felt when she found a group of people who cared about each other? Think about Shannon's example and how she stayed true to her values by creating a new business and selecting the type of customer she served.

- ✓ Write a full profile, describing the type of boss you want leading you, co-workers you want surrounding you and customers you want to serve. Use the following questions as prompts to get you started.

Boss

- ☐ What characteristics do you admire in a leader?
- ☐ How do you want your boss to treat you? Do you need a lot of direction, or more trust and autonomy?

- [ ] Do you prefer to be your own boss or to work for yourself?

Co-Workers

- [ ] How many people do you like to work with? Do you work alone, with a partner, or on a team?
- [ ] How closely do you interact with them?
- [ ] What type of people do you work with?
- [ ] What skills and abilities do you most respect in co-workers?
- [ ] Are they good team players?
- [ ] Are they supportive?

Customers

- [ ] What kind of people do you most like to serve?
- [ ] Do you enjoy having a lot of interaction with your customers, or more indirect contact?

Places

What type of space and atmosphere fits your personality and talents?

Think about the unique offices at Googleplex and how the Internet is changing how and where we work. Remember Julia's story and how her desire to laugh and have fun resulted in her completely changing the atmosphere she worked in. Don't forget Tim Ferriss's suggestion of a four-hour work week when considering your ideal work schedule.

Physical Space

Draw a picture (either in your mind or on a piece of paper) of your ideal workspace.

- [ ] What kind of space do you thrive in?
- [ ] Do you need lots of natural light or windows?

- ☐ Do you need a formal office? Do you prefer working outside, or on your couch?
- ☐ What other details inspire your creativity, influence your mood, and impact your productivity?

Atmosphere

Close your eyes and visualize how you want to *feel* when you are at work.

- ☐ Is your environment serious and formal, or is it more casual and friendly?
- ☐ Does your natural personality shine in this environment, or are you tempering who you really are?

Timing

Print a copy of a month from your calendar and write down your ideal work schedule.

- ☐ How many hours per day do you work?
- ☐ What time of day are you most productive?
- ☐ Which days are workdays, and which are blocked for other parts of your life?
- ☐ What does your ideal calendar include?

Compensation

How do you like to be compensated for your work?

Money is one way, but certainly not the only way, to be compensated for your work. In your ideal scenario, consider how financial rewards compare to recognition and opportunities for growth and development.

- ☐ Create a list outlining how you want to be compensated for your time, creative efforts, and talent.
  - ✓ Remember to include financial awards like money, stock options, and other perks.

- ☐ Describe how you like to be recognized, detailing whether or not awards and notoriety motivate you.
  - ✓ Include any specific information about your desires for continued growth and development.

Expression

Are you able to fully express yourself in your work?

Karrie was unable to express her autonomy as a teacher in the confines of government education. Her frustration led her to create a new environment in which she could really be herself and stretch her ability to help her students. Jessica found it extremely difficult to sell products she didn't believe in. Wanting to help people in an open, honest way eventually led her to open her own business.

- ☐ Are you able to creatively express yourself at work?
- ☐ Do you have the autonomy you require to be your best self?
- ☐ Do the values of the company you work for, the people you work with, and the customers you serve align with your own?

Your environment doesn't have to limit you. Consider for a moment that your education, your experience, and your current environment have nothing to do with what you *could* be doing. Use the FabFinders' examples to open your mind to what is possible and look for more examples that might be closely related to your interests. Consider your answers to the questions above, and start to design your own ideal environment.

Section III: Payoffs

The journey is the reward.

Chinese Proverb

"What? You're kidding, right?" said the collective group of disappointed winners. Had they known the prize was going to be a measly fabric ribbon and short-lived bragging rights, I'm not sure they would have played. I can't say that I even recall what the game was, but boy, do I remember their reactions!

To be fair, their response may have been justified, if not by good manners, then by years of experience. More often than not, the corporation we worked for rewarded us handsomely with money, electronic gadgets, gift certificates, and trips to exotic locations, so I could understand why this group of sales representatives was more than a little surprised to find that they would be getting none of the typical rewards for participating in the most recent "team building" experience. After all, we were in sales; incentives were par for the course, and a ribbon didn't cut it.

So what would have "cut it" for them? What makes playing a particular game worth the energy and effort? In life, what makes taking a new path worth the risks? One of the burning questions I had for the FabFinders was, "Is it worth it?" After risking their seemingly successful careers, disappointing (or at least surprising) their friends and family, and essentially starting from scratch, was the payoff worth it? Is the grass *actually* greener on the other side?

In order to answer this question, I quickly came to realize that "greener" is a relative term. The very phrase implies your view of the colour will be the same once you cross over to "the other side." What I came to understand is that the FabFinders' definitions of success had evolved so much as a result of their journeys that it was nearly impossible to make the comparison. How would their *new* selves ever be able to explain the difference to their *old* (pre-journey) selves?

How would a marketing manager compare the value of her meagre salary to her former *insomniac-lawyer* self, after a decent night's sleep? What words would the Internet blogging entrepreneur use to describe the legacy he was building to his previous *successfully-working-for-daddy's-company* self? How does an author relate the asset of his best-selling book to his former *I-own-a-ski-school* self?

In this last section, we will discuss how the FabFinders measured, determined, and celebrated the outcome of their choices.

Payoffs along the Path:

- **Success**

- **Happiness**

Perhaps challenging the status quo here more than anywhere else, they redefined what it means to be successful and came up with new equations for happiness along the way.

Whether or not you agree with their newfound ambitions or relate to their desires, the stories presented in these last two chapters are meant to challenge you. It's up to you to decide why you're going down this path of *Finding Fabulous* and what will make it worthwhile. Ultimately, you are the one who has to determine what *fabulous* means in your life, and consider how you will know when you find it.

What does fabulous mean to you?

What will make this journey *worth it*?

Chapter 7: Signs of Success

*If you don't know where you are going,
you'll end up someplace else.*

Yogi Berra

Have you ever seen the *Friends* episode in which Chandler and Joey play a game called "Cups"? In an effort to give Joey money without wounding his pride, Chandler invents a card game. With each hand they play, Chandler makes up random rules, and eventually Joey "wins" $1500. Joey has no idea the game is fake, or even why he keeps winning the hands. However, later in the show, he ends up losing all of the money to Ross, playing the same fictitious game. The audience is left wondering how he could play the game, let alone lose so badly, when he didn't even know the rules.

Although the plot of this particular sitcom episode was meant simply as entertainment, I have to wonder if somewhere between the laugh tracks there is a lesson to be found. I start to think about my own journey of Finding Fabulous, and I wonder if I have been as naive as Joey was. For years, I played a similar fictitious game, one for which someone else made up the rules. Despite having more insight than Joey as to the origin of the rules, I still let them determine if I won or lost. I let them define my success.

I set goals according to their bottom line projections and developed my career according to their talent-planning templates. I was enticed by incentives like fitness subsidies and upgraded company cars, and lured toward loyalty by vesting stock options, with little consideration for how much I wanted any of it. When I realized that I was staying for all the wrong reasons, I knew their rules had become my proverbial Golden Handcuffs. Essentially, I was playing a corporate game of "Cups."

As I became more fascinated by the stories of the FabFinders, I also became curious about this concept of success. What did success look like outside those corporate walls? What did success mean for people who started defining it for themselves? Perhaps the sceptics I spoke to—the ones who wanted to know if the FabFinders were successful—instigated my curiosity even more than the actual FabFinders. Whether spoken or implied, the sceptics usually meant, "Do they make any money doing that?" So *I* wanted to know. I wanted to know if this brave leap of faith toward finding more meaning, purpose, and fun had more of a measure than a mere dollar sign. Is there more to success than just money? How does one know if she is truly successful? Does the idea of success evolve throughout the transformation, and if so, how?

One of the more surprising things about the FabFinders' responses was the difficulty some of them had with remembering their previous definitions of success. Most, if not all, of them seemed to have a very clear definition about what success means for them today. However, when I asked how that changed throughout their transformation, a few of them were stumped. They said, "I don't *know* what it was before," or, "I *guess* it was …" They tossed out things like six-figure salaries, big promotions, a big house, or a fancy car, but it seemed like they were stretching for an answer. It appeared they had never really taken the time to figure out the answer for themselves.

As I pieced together the relevance of their admissions, I came to the conclusion that it was time to stop playing someone else's game and start making my own rules. In that vein, the FabFinders offered me three important components for creating my own equation of success.

Chapter 7: Signs of Success

- **Identify Influencing Factors**
- **Redefine What It Means to Be Successful**
- **Recognize and Celebrate**

I firmly believe in the old adage, "Success is a journey, not a destination," so it is my wish that you learn to find success along your journey of Finding Fabulous; don't wait to reach some presupposed destination. It is not my intention to decide what your success will look like or to suppose it will look anything like mine. I simply hope the FabFinders' examples and newfound descriptions help you come up with your own definition.

Identify Influencing Factors

> *Think twice before you speak, because your words and influence will plant the seed of either success or failure in the mind of another.*
>
> **Napoleon Hill**

In Canada, we have this crazy obsession with the game of hockey. I say crazy obsession because I've been in the arenas and witnessed the passion of the hockey moms and dads. They jump up and down, yell at the refs, and even fight with each other on occasion. Success, for those parents, is all about the amount of ice time their kids get, the percentage of time they touch the puck, and how many times they put it in the net. How much fun the child has or whether they forge strong friendships seems somewhat secondary (or tertiary) to more tangible evidence of success. Despite the fact that some enlightened parents and coaches may preach the value of teamwork and the importance of leadership, those qualities do not appear in the stats records or on the scoreboard. After all, those things won't land their kids in the NHL.

What if that wasn't the case? Imagine for a moment that minor hockey associations started keeping stats based on different metrics. How would players answer the question, "How successful were you at hockey this season?" Can you imagine them quoting the number of friends they made or how much their self-confidence grew, instead of reciting their win/loss record or their team's place in the annual tournament? Or imagine that at the start of the season players were asked what they wanted to get out of their experience. Then, at the end of the season, they could grade themselves on their attainment of "success." Think of how they could translate that to the rest of their lives.

Obviously, sports like hockey (or soccer, baseball, football, etc.) measure success with a scoreboard; after all, that's the object of the game. I'm a fairly competitive person myself, so I'm not proposing that we do away with the concept of winning and losing. I guess I'm just suggesting that there is benefit in digging a little deeper to understand what else makes us feel successful. Aside from numbers on a scoreboard, how do we know we've succeeded?

When I played competitive sports as a child, I judged my own success on my ability to win. Thinking back on what made me feel successful, I remember the number of trophies I won in baseball and which ribbons I earned in gymnastics. For me, the greatest influence was the external validation I received from winning.

As I compared various FabFinders' earlier definitions of success, I uncovered more common influences. A dream-building coach told me her definition of success was impacted by her father's opinion of what was appropriate (i.e., enough) for her. A marketing executive told me her idea of success was to fulfill her family's expectations and make them proud. A singer shared her longing to be well known and loved by the public, and a PR executive found success in praise from her clients.

Even though our experiences varied greatly, it seemed that our early ideas of success were most influenced by our role models, society as a whole, and external validation we received along the way.

Perhaps if we take a closer look and get really honest about what's made us feel successful in the past, we can stop caring so much about whether other people think we are successful and simply concentrate on whether or not *we* do.

Role Models

> *What you do speaks so loudly that I cannot hear what you say.*
>
> Ralph Waldo Emerson

Parents don't have to be screaming at a hockey game to have their actions speak louder than their words. I spoke to a psychiatrist whose father staged an intervention when his son considered turning down his medical school acceptance to become a stand-up comic. Jacqueline realized that she became a lawyer only because it was what her mother had always wanted. And although Beena didn't become a doctor, her family's esteem for the profession made a lasting impact on her: in order to compensate for her choices, she spent the majority of her career trying to become successful according to corporate America's standards.

Uniquely, Pierrette's example was almost completely opposite to the other FabFinders in terms of meeting parental expectations. Her story is a great example of how, despite those early influencers, we can choose who we allow to impact us as we endeavour to find our own versions of success.

Pierrette's Story

> *How does a child who was never encouraged to pursue her dreams end up becoming a dream-builder who helps others attain theirs?*
>
> *As a child, Pierrette always dreamed of being a teacher. She laughed as she told me her siblings wouldn't play schoolhouse with her because she always insisted on being the teacher. Her father, however, had somewhat antiquated views about the whether women need higher education. Being a waitress was about the highest expectation he held for her, so Pierrette did what was expected and got a job straight out of high school. It isn't too surprising to me when she explains how she used her job as an employment placement specialist to help people*

find their dream jobs. Perhaps being steered away from that herself gave her the extra drive to ensure that didn't happen to others.

A few years later, her desire for more financial freedom led her to become an independent consultant for Mary Kay. She explains how Mary Kay was a huge influence on her definition of success in those days. First, the founder stressed the importance of prioritizing success in the order of God, Family, and Career, instilling the belief that if you were successful in the first two, the latter would take care of itself. However, at the time Pierrette was more influenced by the incentives the company offered, like the pink Cadillac and financial rewards. She wanted the money, the car, and the big house! Two years later, after reaching her goals, she ran out of things to accomplish. In essence, she forgot to keep dreaming.

Around the same time, Pierrette's childhood influences reared their heads when she decided to get married. She thought she'd have a good life as a wife and mother, so she wouldn't need anything else. Despite that belief, something inside her still longed to be realized.

Although Pierrette told me about interim jobs she took in radio advertising and retail sales, it was her experience with a life coach that seemed to influence her ideas of success the most. Her mentor, John C. Maxwell, taught her that our ideas about success are limited by how our mentors define it. She learned that she needed to surround herself with people who inspired her to keep dreaming bigger.

Even after years of working hard to overcome the beliefs introduced by her father, Pierrette still struggles to feel worthy of the success she dreams of. When she was younger, she thought success meant doing things the way her dad did them. Now that she's finally realized that isn't true, she feels free to be more creative and to tap into what God intends for her. She's learned that it's possible to respect someone else's idea of success without having to agree with it. Unless someone is already at the level of success she wants for herself, she doesn't listen to his or her opinion on what she "should" do.

As she describes her path today, she goes back to the pillars of success she learned at Mary Kay. She believes that if she is at peace with her God, knowing she is living the purpose she was meant to live, and if she surrounds herself with family members who support her progress, her career will be successful too. With that confidence and clarity of purpose, Pierrette has in turn become a role model and mentor for her clients as they, too, learn to keep dreaming bigger.

The lesson I appreciate most from Pierrette's story is the power of intentionality. She didn't have a say in what her father thought about success, but she did eventually learn to find encouragement from a different source. In addition, she recognized when certain role models were capping her vision of possible, and she was able to go out and find new inspiration. In essence, she redefined success on an ongoing basis, leveraging the success of those around her.

What do the role models in your life think about success? Are you letting their definitions hold you back, or do they motivate you to dream bigger?

Society

If you ask any Canadians where they were at the moment Sydney Crosby "sent one low into the net" to clinch the gold medal for Canada in the 2010 Vancouver Games, chances are they could tell you. It was the "shot heard 'round the country"—one for the record books! Although I'm not sure it was explicitly said on any of the Canadian broadcast stations, I think that goal was worth more than just one gold medal. I believe it was worth fourteen. You see, before the boys laced up their skates for that grand finale, we had already won more gold medals than any other host country in the history of the Winter Games. By all accounts, we were already successful. However, it wasn't until that red light flashed behind the net, nearly eight minutes into overtime, that we as a country could celebrate.

Now I'm not suggesting the Vancouver Games would have been a failure if the men's hockey team hadn't won the gold that day, but I am suggesting that the degree of success would have been overshadowed. Hockey is, after all, one of our national sports, and most undoubtedly stirs our national pride. It would have been a crying shame if that game had gone the other way, not just for the members of that team, but for every single athlete who had won medals up to that point. The media would have turned quickly, forgetting all about those earlier successes and shifting all the airtime to conversations about the one that got away. Luckily for those athletes (and perhaps, in a way, for all of us), we'll never know if my prediction would have come true, because on that day, at that minute, in that glorious moment, we were given permission to cheer!

Just like the fevered anticipation of that hockey game, society can have a huge impact on how we think and feel. Public opinion plays a huge role, above and beyond the influence our parents and other role models have on our ideas about success. Although she "played" in an altogether different "arena," Twila was also impacted by society's definition of success. As is fairly common in the world of entertainment, Twila thought success was defined by fame and fortune. She thought the ultimate level of success was to be well-known for your talent, and to be highly paid for it.

Twila's Story

With a contract deal from Atlantic Records in her hands, it seemed that Twila was well on her way to achieving the fame and fortune she sought. Little did she know just how differently she would view that definition of success thirty years later: "I think the most famous and wealthy people are the most screwed up!" What happened? Why the change of heart?

When Twila was young, her family always knew she was meant for the stage. They would find her in her room, lining up every doll and teddy bear she could find in front of her giant chalkboard. She would stand in front of her captive audience, telling them elaborate stories and presenting all kinds of ideas. So it didn't come as much of a surprise when her family discovered that, at the age of thirteen, Twila had a beautiful singing voice. They figured she was meant to tell those stories through song, and supported her dream to become a professional singer.

Eight years later, her dreams seemed to be coming true. However, when she arrived in Los Angeles to start her contract, she found out she was pregnant with her daughter, which violated a clause in her contract that stated she wasn't allowed to get pregnant for the first five years. This effectively ended Twila's singing career before it ever began. Heading back home with her tail between her legs, she accepted an offer to work for her aunt's real estate business. She ended up spending the next twenty years climbing the ladder of "success" in sales and marketing. That success led her to work for some of the most prestigious condo properties on the Las Vegas Strip.

Although she was quite successful by external standards, she still longed to express herself creatively. One day a colleague remarked that the gift baskets Twila made for her clients were so beautiful that she could start her own company, so she did. Initially, that business gave Twila the creative outlet she was looking for, allowing her to spend most of her time planning new creations. However, the near crash of that business, followed by a major rebounding growth spurt, resulted in Twila's spending more time on the business end of things and less time on the creations. No longer able to find joy in her work, Twila decided it was time to sell her business to a competitor, and closed up shop.

Her return to Las Vegas, along with a brief second stint as a marketer in the real estate business, led Twila to her current role. As she met more women entrepreneurs at networking events, she realized just how valuable her business failures and successes had been. Finding her voice once again, Twila explains, "No one was teaching these women how to run profitable businesses."

Today, as she builds her speaking and coaching business, she is clearer about the impact she wants to make. "When I was a singer, it was never about the music. I was always trying to connect with the audience and change their moment," she says. Now she wants to connect with her customers and change their perceptions of what's possible. Her success is based on enlightening entrepreneurs, whether or not that brings her fame and fortune.

> *She ends the interview by summing up her newfound definition of success: "The other day my daughter posted to her Facebook that I am the most wonderful mom in the world. That is all the fame I need to feel successful!"*

Working in the entertainment industry, it probably isn't too surprising that Twila initially saw fame and fortune as reasonable markers for success. After all, how often do you hear about entertainers who aren't famous and don't make any money, but they're super-happy and fulfilled? Those stories just don't make the evening news. We are more apt to hear about who makes the most money or who has the most Twitter followers. Although she had to remove herself from the environment that influenced her definition, Twila was able to figure out a new way to measure her accomplishments. Perhaps it's a bit of sweet justice, knowing the daughter who effectively ended Twila's run at fame and fortune ended up providing her with the only source of fame she ever needed.

How much has society impacted your views on success? Are you letting collective popular opinion dictate whether or not you are successful?

External Validation

Back in the day, the NHL was known for bringing in enforcers (a.k.a. "goons") to protect their star players (think Probert, McSorley, and Domi). These were the players known for their brawling skills more than anything else. Although today the tougher players seem to also have some mean hockey skills, I believe the practice is still quite common in lower-level leagues. I wonder what kind of goals these players have for themselves and if they define success differently from the top scorers. What does success mean to these players? Have their experiences guided them in a different direction? The first time they ever fought, were they rewarded with pats on the back and new admiration from their teammates? Did they "fight" their way onto the roster of the best teams?

Thinking about the loud, cheering crowds that erupt every time the gloves are dropped. It's not hard to imagine how a hard-won fight might be considered a sort of success. Whether or not we agree with the inclusion of

Chapter 7: Signs of Success

fighting in the sport, how can we expect anything different from these players if they have always been rewarded for their acts?

Even though we live our lives outside the hockey arena, are we that dissimilar? How much have the "cheering crowds" impacted our ideas about success? Even if we had the most liberal role models encouraging us to define success for ourselves, and we could remain unaffected by the views of society, what role do our personal experiences play in our overall equation of success? Like the aggressive hockey player, are we being shaped and moulded by the reactions to our actions?

Growing up, I remember being rewarded most for my grades in school. Although I didn't always get straight A's, I got my fair share. It was the main way I knew I was successful. To get as many A's as I could, I became very good at following instructions and figuring out just what the teacher wanted. This worked quite well for me, with the exception of the teacher I told you about earlier. Once I was in a classroom that substituted the value of creativity and innovation for conventional grading norms, I struggled to understand what was expected of me. As you know, the end result earned me the description of "not very creative," and instilled a self-limiting belief for years afterward.

Reflecting on that experience now, I can see how I attempted to replace those grades with other tangible evidence of success. As a waitress, I was obsessed with the percentage of tips I made, naively thinking my aptitude for serving was the only factor in customers' decisions to be generous or not. As a sales rep, I not only wanted to exceed my sales quotas, I also wanted to exceed expectations on my performance appraisals. Looking back on it now, I see how my constant need for approval from other people prevented me from succeeding at anything for the pure joy of it. It prevented me from even attempting goals that weren't attached to some sort of "grade."

Like me, Lara sought out the opinions of others to determine whether or not she was successful—a tactic that worked really well until she had a baby.

a baby changed my DNA," she states matter-of-factly, ₁g what instigated her career (and more importantly, her life) transformation. For nearly a decade, Lara's extroverted personality seemed to make her a perfect fit for a corporate job in communications and PR. The lucrative salary allowed her to enjoy a nice apartment in the city, and gave her discretionary income to do the things she enjoyed, like dining out and travelling. I hear the joy in her voice as she reflects back on that time: "I thought it was the pinnacle of my success."

She tells me her definition of success included being surrounded by friends and family, travelling, and doing what she wanted, when she wanted. She also discloses that she felt most successful when she was rewarded and acknowledged for her work, especially all the times clients sent notes of praise to her boss or took her out to dinner in appreciation for her efforts. Pay raises and promotions were frequent, adding to the validation she received. Life was pretty good.

Then she had a baby. To her surprise, Lara's priorities shifted in a major way. All of a sudden, that corporate life she used to love didn't seem to fit with her role as a mom. The business didn't stop for sick babies or sleep-deprived mothers. The decision to leave that organization to stay home and raise her children led to even more surprises. Lara didn't realize just how much her psyche relied on external rewards and recognition to feel successful. As a mom, she was doing the hardest job of her life, but no one was acknowledging her. As she describes it, "There was no clear path to success, no job was ever finished, and there was nothing to reflect back on to see if you did a good job."

Struggling to feel like she was making some type of contribution, or to see the triumph in being a mom, Lara sought the help of a coach. It was only then that she came to understand that she was never

Chapter 7: Signs of Success

going to be able to measure success the way she used to before. Th acknowledgement was a huge milestone.

Describing the baby steps she had to take to find a new way of articulating what success meant for her, she tells me it started off with being able to take a shower five days a week or getting twenty minutes of uninterrupted time to herself. These tiny accomplishments signalled a huge shift from the size of the goals she used to set in her working career, yet on some days they were no less difficult to achieve. With time and perspective, Lara has also come to understand how she used to seek validation for doing great work on things that held little meaning for her personally.

Now, as a business coach and entrepreneur, Lara has created a source for the external validation she was missing. The ability to help other women define their own parameters of success has been one of the most rewarding aspects of her job. She says it's one of the most difficult mind shifts a new entrepreneur makes.

I can't help wondering if her former colleagues would change their opinions of Lara "sacrificing her career" or "giving it all up" in order to raise her family. It seems to me that Lara's definition of success may have changed as a result, but in no way has her accomplishment of it.

There were no cheering crowds to help Lara figure out if she was doing motherhood right or making all kinds of mistakes. She had to learn not only to set new goals and ambitions *for* herself, but also to receive validation *from* herself. Her story is a great lesson in the fact that success is not something that is awarded to us by someone else. Success is something we give to ourselves – a gift that helps us chart our course and celebrate our journey.

Are you waiting for someone else to "grade" you before you feel successful? If the only validation you would ever receive in the future had to come from you, how would that change the way you approach success in your life?

Redefine What It Means To Be Successful

*If you don't design your own life plan,
chances are you'll fall into someone else's plan.
And guess what they have planned for you? Not much.*

Jim Rohn

Do you think someone can spend her entire life in poverty and still be considered successful? What if she had no personal belongings to her name, and spent her days walking amongst the poorest of the poor? Would she be considered successful? Before you answer, I want to remind you of a little (in stature, not influence) woman named Mother Teresa. By any definition of material wealth, no one would have considered her rich, but do you think there is a soul on this Earth who would say she wasn't successful?

I'm sure if Mother Teresa were here, she would say it doesn't matter. I obviously didn't know the woman personally, but I can't for the life of me imagine that she ever used someone else's definition of success to guide her decisions. She is perhaps the quintessential example of someone who lived on her own terms and redefined success along the way.

Throughout this process of Finding Fabulous, this is one of the most important lessons I have learned: define your own success. As simple as that sounds, I admit I had no idea how to do it. Even today, I continue to struggle with what that means for me. I struggle to defend my evolving definition to the naysayers. I struggle to acknowledge it to myself and I struggle to celebrate it regularly. Don't get me wrong—I'm getting better than I ever was, but it isn't as easy as it might sound.

Attempting to understand how the FabFinders went about redefining success on their own terms, I asked them to describe their process. Interestingly enough, some of them spoke of life-changing events, like motherhood and near-death experiences, that brought new perspective on what was most important to them. Others were awakened when they realized that the people they were striving to emulate were externally successful, yet they were miserable internally. Many spoke of realizing how they had forgotten to re-evaluate their definitions of success over the years.

This is where I found the greatest lessons for defining my own success. If I could clarify what I wanted my success to look like, separate from anyone else's, and if I could find a way to check in and re-evaluate it on a regular basis, perhaps I would be more likely to attain it.

How do you define success? Are you creating a definition based on the success of those around you? Has a major event in your life transformed what is important to you? Have you come to realize that success today means something different than it used to?

Define Your Own Success: Stop the Comparison Game

> *Your time is limited, so don't waste it living someone else's life. Don't be trapped by dogma, which is living with the results of other people's thinking. Don't let the noise of others' opinions drown out your own inner voice. Most important, have the courage to follow your heart and intuition.*
>
> **Steve Jobs**

How high does a fish fly? How fast does a bird swim? Can you imagine comparing the success of a bird to that of a fish? How ridiculous is that?!? Just because a bird can fly better than a fish, does that make it any more successful?

It is amazing what happens when you decide to define success for yourself. You get to work toward things you actually care about that make you feel good. But above and beyond that, it frees you from comparing your success to others. How can you possibly compare yourself to someone else when there is almost no chance that your equations of success are exactly the same? We want such different combinations of similar things—and at various levels or degrees—that it's nearly impossible to compare our success to that of others. So why bother?

Darren's Story

The FabFinders validated this point as they described how they had to stop comparing themselves to others in order to redefine their own success. Darren was working at an exclusive fitness club when he figured this out for himself.

"They had big bank accounts, but their lives were so messed up!" Darren tells me, recalling his work training the rich clientele at a premier fitness club. He admits that, at the time, his idea of success was tied to acquiring things—things he never had growing up. That remained true until he started to spend his days with very wealthy businessmen. Despite the fact that they seemed to have everything Darren was working hard to get, they were miserable! Compared to them, Darren had little money or resources, yet he was able to make a positive impact on their lives. "I was just a personal trainer, and yet I'm helping them triple their sales and grow their businesses," he says, shaking his head at the memory.

That realization shifted Darren's mindset about how he viewed success. He stopped trying to acquire status and respect through material possessions and started to focus on the impact he was making. He even went as far as declaring his new intention by writing "I will not be defined by my title" on his locker at the club. Although he held firmly to the belief he didn't need a title in order to have the impact he wanted, the environment and hierarchal structure of the club put a ceiling on what he believed he could accomplish. That environment eventually caused him to leave and open his own gym.

With that, Darren had the autonomy he needed to define success on his own terms. As he describes it, "My vision of success is how much value I can add to other people's lives." Eventually that vision led him to create a specialized fitness program in the private school his four boys attended. In addition to the physical benefits, the program had an impact on the children's self-esteem, confidence, and grade levels; this gave Darren his next undertaking. He now believes his mission is to influence the lives of young people so they think about themselves the right way, regardless of what environment they come from.

> *His goal is to bring his program to public schools across the province, and he's hoping to help kids define success on their own terms.*
>
> *I guess you could say Darren's story brought him full circle. Growing up in a difficult environment taught him to compare his success to other people, whereas now he teaches children in those same situations how to define success for themselves.*

Just as we can't compare a bird to a fish, we can't compare our attainment of success to others, because we can't assume they are striving to achieve the same things that we are. Darren learned that the external success he saw in the businessmen he trained was attached to internal misery. He wanted the former, not the latter.

Thinking about what this means for my own life, I realize there is no one who has or wants exactly the same things I do. I want the huge, beautiful cottage down by the lake, but not the lifestyle that prevents its owner from using it regularly. I want the frequent flyer miles of the CEO I see sitting in First Class, but I don't want to work for the corporate giant that he does. My success means having a smaller, more humble cottage that I use all the time and sitting in First Class to travel the world doing inspiring work. Does that make me more or less successful than the other two? Perhaps the cottage owner isn't at his cottage because his idea of success is spending more time on the golf course. Or maybe the CEO's idea of success is being the best leader that organization has ever had. Who's more successful in this scenario? See, it's the bird-versus-fish quandary all over again: you can't compare them.

Aside from the above-mentioned dangers associated with playing the comparison game, I do admit there is some value in looking around to see what "success" looks like (whatever *you* define that to be). Wanting something similar to someone else's "success" can give you valuable clues to what your ideal life would look like. Just remember to decipher your full equation based on what's important to you, and don't measure your attainment of success based on others' formulas.

How would your life look and feel if you abolished any need to compare your *success* to that of others?

Definitions Evolve: Re-evaluate Often

> *She's the kind of girl who climbed the ladder of success wrong by wrong.*
>
> Mae West

The FabFinders made it abundantly clear to me that our ideas of success change. They didn't claim to be forced into doing what they did or that they never wanted what they got. In fact, it was quite the opposite. More often I heard that they stopped asking themselves what they wanted or forgot to evaluate whether they were getting it. The architect was always fascinated with the design of things; it just took ten years to realize he was more interested in the design of the people who filled the buildings rather than the buildings themselves. The radio producer was always interested in sharing stories; she just took twenty years to figure out she'd rather spread good ones. The greatest insight seemed to lie in the re-evaluation of their successes. Forget to do that for too many years, and we forget why we started down the path in the first place.

One of the first interviews I did was with Tanya, the radio producer who told me she "climbed the corporate ladder only to realize it was leaning against the wrong wall." Although I understood the point she was trying to make, it made me wonder if there are ever any "wrong ladders" to climb. I'll wax philosophical for a moment and suggest that perhaps everything we do is for a reason; every step we take teaches us something new and brings us closer to where we are meant to go. Do you believe that?

After listening to so many of the FabFinders connect the dots of their life, I believe it now more than ever. Considering how well the golf pro translates her golf skills to the business world, I can't see running her family business as a misstep on her career ladder. I think about the horse therapist whose talent was only strengthened by her engineering background, along with the writer whose psychology degree helps her dig to the heart of her subject's story. As for my own path to this point in my journey, I can only view my time in the corporate world as preparation for what's to come.

Even though I believe there is a purpose in doing the things that bring us to this point, I also believe we wait too long to get here. A common, yet unspoken, truth weaving through the majority of the interviews was the fact that many of us decided what we wanted to be when we grew up, but we forget to check in along the way. How often do we look up to see what ladder we are climbing and ask ourselves if we still want to be on it? How often do we take the time to scan the horizon for other ladders in order to know if we are ready to jump? As we grow and evolve, so do our wants and ambitions, so it is a good idea to make a habit out of checking on our progress.

It never ceased to amaze me how the FabFinders could casually throw out a life-threatening brain bleed, a car accident, or kidney failure as the catalyst for re-evaluating their definitions of success. Before I had time to close my mouth and regain my composure, they had usually already moved on to the "it was the best thing that ever happened to me" part of the conversation. Really? I mean, I can understand the accompanying sense of gratitude for life, but I have a harder time understanding why it takes such a drastic event. Why do we wait until the worst of the worst happens before we take stock of our lives?

How has your definition of success evolved along the way, and what might it be telling you about your future? Do you evaluate your definition of success on a regular basis? If not, what are you waiting for?

Recognize & Celebrate Success

One of the most enviable things Lara told me during our time together was how clear she was on whether she was successful. As you learned from her story, she has defined those parameters very intentionally. However, what I found even more interesting was how she measures them. Perhaps the most impressive way Lara measures success is by her ability to have a healthy, home-cooked meal on the table by 6:30 on at least five nights every week. That goal is actually written in her business plan! Fairly typical of a strategic businessperson, Lara also has specific numbers that help her monitor whether her business is growing the way she wants: the growth of her revenue and the number of clients, compared with her desired targets. But Lara has determined that family is her number one priority, and she believes keeping it that way has a positive impact on her business.

Lara's mealtime ritual is a great indicator that she is staying grounded and playing at the top of her game. Highlighting her commitment, Lara told me how tough it was to shut down her computer during the week she was trying to launch two programs. However, she knew she had to do it in order to maintain her integrity. How could she expect her clients to be accountable for their own success if she wasn't being a role model? At the same time, she knows she is teaching her children that it's possible to love your job and be successful at it without neglecting the rest of your life to pursue it.

I think Lara is on to something with respect to measuring success. I love how simple her indicator is and that it offers her a daily reminder of her biggest priority. It makes me wonder how I can adapt the practice in my own life. Staying healthy and fit is high on my list of priorities. My physical strength and stamina are key to my ability to accomplish everything else in my life; if I slack in those areas, everything from my mood to my motivation suffers. Given the impact I know it has on the rest of my goals, a good indicator of my success could be how much physical exercise I get in a day. If I can start my day off with a great workout, I know my day will be a success. Whether I get anything accomplished or not, I know I'll feel great, both physically and mentally.

If I learned nothing else from the FabFinders, I came away with one important lesson: work and life goals don't have to be separate. In fact, it seemed they were often intertwined and codependent. As much as my conversations started out discussing major career shifts, they inevitably landed on the life transformations that happened along the way. Every time I asked for someone's definition of success, they brought up things like impacting the world, feeling happy, and spending time with their children. Did they have other work-related goals? Sure. But it seemed the true measure of success took them beyond the borders between work and life. Lara's goal isn't just to make dinner; she firmly believes it impacts her ability to be successful in business. She wasn't the only FabFinder to consider success in one area of their life a catalyst or keystone for another.

As I consider this phenomenon, I realize that it's part of the reason I call this a journey of Finding Fabulous. It isn't about finding your ideal job or fixing your home life, it's about finding your *best* life. Work is a component, bu apparently, the place where fabulous is found, becomes inseparable from the rest.

Recognizing Success: A New Equation

> *The more you praise and celebrate your life,
> the more there is in life to celebrate.*
>
> **Oprah Winfrey**

Beyond the formalized, structured definition tied to my former title, I had to figure out what success looks like. For so many years, I had an actual number tied to that definition; I was in sales, after all. Success meant hitting a specific number. I had a number to reach for sales expectations, a number for the percentage of growth my products achieved, and a number for how many interactions I had with my customers. My success was written in numbers, at least according to the organization I worked for. Did I want more in terms of success? Sure. I wanted to be learning and growing. I wanted to be a good teammate and have the respect of my customers. I just never tied that to my definition of success. I never gave those other parameters their due attention.

Like everyone else, I'd heard a thousand times how important it was to set goals. I intuitively knew my ability to achieve them would increase if I merely wrote them down. What escaped me for so many of those years was how important it was to define them for myself. Setting a sales target because my company wanted it was not enough. Thinking about where my career might be in a few years didn't cut it. What else did I want for myself? How did I see my bigger impact on the world? What did I want my relationships to look like? Who did I want to be?

One of the people who really brought this issue home for me was a man I met at a conference. He led the entire event with such a ridiculous amount of energy and exuded such an unexpected, calm sense of inner peace that I couldn't help but be in awe of him. That awe was only heightened when

.t he was a devoted Yogi, corporate genius, and father of three. Seriously? How did he manage all of that?

almost as unique as he is; in fact, he was the one FabFinder who hadn't left his corporate job. Despite finding himself in a place similar to the rest of us, K.C. did what most people might think impossible (or at least improbable): he created his own job within the company he worked for.

K.C.'s Story

As K.C. describes the culture at the digital media advertising company he works for, it isn't too surprising to hear that, when he was toying with the idea of leaving, he was advised to stay. Pride lights up his face as he tells me the company has won top awards, for multiple years in a row, as the best place to work in America. He admits to always feeling blessed to work in a location of his choosing, with the full trust of his company and without being micromanaged by his boss. Despite all of the reasons he should stay, including the fact that he has a wife and three children to feed, K.C. struggled to feel aligned with his day-to-day role as regional director of sales.

Taking advantage of a three-week sabbatical, K.C. decided to do what he calls "radical introspection and self-care." He completely shut himself off from e-mail and the Internet to spend hours each day meditating, running trails, and journaling. The result of that focused time and energy was a personal manifesto that would change the course of K.C.'s career and provide a framework for the integration of his entire life.

In that framework, K.C. came up with what he calls his "nonnegotiables": soul, vitality, family, art, and career. In an effort to integrate those nonnegotiables, he also created a completely new job description, along with a case for why he should become the company's "National Director of Sales Energy." Combining a strong talent for motivating and inspiring sales reps with his passion for personal development, along with his prior experience as a sales rep, K.C. believed he could make a bigger impact on the company's performance while gaining the freedom to express his creativity.

Chapter 7: Signs of Success

> *The pure bravery that must have taken is evident as K.C. de_ walking in to the VP's office with a strong sense that he was about to be fired.*
>
> *Fortunately for him, and I suspect for his company, they were willing to negotiate the terms for K.C.'s new role. Although they chose to give him the more traditional title of "Education and Development Strategist," K.C. now spends his days consulting with the executives of the company on major issues and developing communication and educational training programs. Colleagues often refer to him as the culture catalyst and torch bearer as his innovative methods have impacted the company in fun and unique ways, including the addition of meditation training and "presencing" practices.*

Far beyond the benefits of helping him find a new job, I think K.C.'s framework offers a simple, effective way for the rest of us to define and recognize success, both in and out of work situations. If you have ever heard the term work–life balance and wondered what the heck that actually means, you are not alone. I'm pretty sure the Blackberry killed the notion for me. How do you balance the time and energy you spend at work with the time you spend at home if your work is literally clipped to your belt? K.C. redefined the concept as "work-life integration," and strives to live what he calls "the integrated life." To be fair, I'm not sure if he coined the phrase or just a really cool way of implementing it. Either way, it's genius. I'm not sure I can do it proper justice, so I suggest you check it out yourself at www.thisepiclife.com

K.C. explains:

> *I define integration as when you're attempting to fire equally on all cylinders, across all of the nonnegotiable aspects of your life. For me those have been: meditation, vitality, family, art, and work. Work may be last in the order, but it's for good reason. Our work is where we create value for everyone and everything around us. Our work should benefit from the nonnegotiables that come before it, not exist as a separate, tougher "obligation."*

K.C. redefined his own success as the continual expansion of his nonnegotiables, and he strives to become more proficient and to pursue mastery in each one. Although he admits he isn't there yet, he is able to use the framework to guide his decisions and recognize his progress. He knows exactly what makes him feel successful in terms of his meditation practice, the vitality he seeks, and the goals he has for his family life. He creates a priority and definition of success for both his art (i.e., his music) and his work (i.e., his paid day job). The framework guides him to intentionally choose activities and goals that include several of his nonnegotiables. This allows him to bring meditation into his work, art into his family, and vitality into all of it.

Interestingly, as I worked to translate the FabFinders' stories into lessons for the rest of us, I struggled to fit them under the category of work/career. It seemed the more questions I asked about major career shifts, the more I heard about the resulting life transformations. It didn't take long to understand that the two were inseparable. Maybe that's why I love K.C.'s story so much; he intentionally integrates them. I think visionaries like Mother Teresa do the same, removing the line between how they live and what they do for work.

Are you defining your own success? Does that definition create space for everything you want for your life, or merely for your work?

Celebrating Success: Importance of Small Wins

There's this incredible feeling that accompanies a perfectly hit golf ball. The club slices through the air, and it feels almost effortless. But even more amazing than the shot itself is the effect it has afterward. If you've ever been a beginner golfer, you'll know what I mean. Those first few years spent hacking divots out of pristine fairways and hooking balls into the abyss of the fescue are survived by only the memory of that perfect shot. It's as if you can take a hundred horrible shots for every good one. That one great shot keeps your faith alive: "I know I can do it! This one time, I hit such a long, clean shot!" On the road to Finding Fabulous, perhaps the biggest benefit of measuring success regularly is the ability to recognize that one perfect shot and to use the celebration of it to remind you of what's possible.

More than one FabFinder expressed frustration about staying motivated during the tough times in their transitions. It was the recognition of their "perfect shots" that seemed to carry them through it. The former teacher felt anxious about not having enough tutoring students to make her business viable until she switched her focus to the impact she was having on the students she did have. A new golf pro had similar worries in the early days of her business, but she found success in the eyes of her clients and the impact her instruction was having on the rest of their lives.

Katie, the teacher who wanted to be an artist, stressed this lesson about celebrating small wins when she told me her story. Questioning whether she was good enough as an artist to quit her teaching job, Katie took a leap of faith and entered a contest. To her surprise, she won second place. Although it was a small accomplishment, it went a long way toward giving her enough validation and confidence to put her work out there. In essence, it became the perfect shot. That success led her to a job as a book illustrator, and eventually to a position teaching art at a local college. Admitting that she still has self-doubts, she believes that measuring her small successes along the way is what keeps her moving toward her dream.

As I reflect on my own journey toward Finding Fabulous, I remember how difficult it was to do that. Since I didn't know what I wanted to do, and I often felt like I was in limbo, I barely knew how to recognize success, let alone measure it. What metrics do you use for that? The lack of an answer prevented me from celebrating anything I did for a long time. It wasn't until I started to share my journey with others that I had a change of perspective. Friends who hadn't drummed up the courage to leave their jobs reminded me how brave my move had been. When I took off for California to write this book, others who were stuck in one of the coldest winters on record told me they were living vicariously through me. Comments and support like that helped remind me that I had a lot to celebrate. I could celebrate finding the inspiration to write a book or the ability to find so many people to share their stories. I could relish all the days I woke up knowing I had complete control over my day, and be grateful for the curiosity that sparked my creative process. There were lots of milestones and signs that I was getting closer and closer to my ideal life, but most of all, there were all kinds of indications that I was already living it.

What do you celebrate regularly to keep you motivated on your journey toward your best life?

Roadmap: Success in Finding Fabulous

My own experience, validated by the people I interviewed, taught me how important it is to challenge what success means to me. Only then could I recognize it when I'd found it.

Now it's your turn. As we've learned from the FabFinders, success in Finding Fabulous requires consideration of these three things:

- **Influencing Factors:** Understanding what influences your thoughts about success
- **Definition:** Importance of redefining success for yourself
- **Recognition:** Importance of celebrating your success along the way

Let's peel back the layers of your **Equation for Success**:

Influencing Factors

Who or what influences your ideas about success?

Remember the societal pressures that had Twila longing for the fame and fortune that came with being a famous singer? With time and greater perspective, she realized her real desire was for a stronger connection with her audience. Then there was Pierrette, who allowed her father's views on what success was supposed to look like for a woman to prevent her from dreaming beyond being a housewife. Before Lara became a mother, she let her co-workers' and clients' validation and approval of her work dictate whether or not she was successful.

- ☐ What does SUCCESS mean? What phrases, images, or thoughts come to your mind when you hear that word?
    - ✓ Take time to write out as many things as you can think of, without worrying too much whether or not these are things you want. This exercise is solely to identify what you see as representing success.

- ☐ Are you letting other people influence your ideas about success?
- ☐ Look back over the list you just made. For each item, ask yourself these three questions:
    - ✓ Is this just popular opinion, or do I believe this? Is there something in today's society (culture, norms, etc.) that causes me to think this?
    - ✓ Do I think this because of something my parents or other role models said or did?
    - ✓ Does this measure of success require approval or validation from someone other than myself?

This exercise is not meant to judge what you see as success. It's intended only to heighten your awareness of why you think the way you do.

Definition

What is your definition of success?

Darren's definition of success started to change when he met wealthy businessmen who seemed to have everything he was working toward, yet they were unhappy. Realizing how empty and broken they were gave him cause to stop comparing himself to others and start redefining what he wanted for his own life. Leaving behind the corporate world, with all the sales targets and defined parameters of success, was a rude awakening for me. All of a sudden I didn't know how to define my success.

What does your definition of success look like?

- ☐ If you aren't sure, consider using a method like K.C.'s (check out his website: www.thisepiclife.com for a more detailed description).
- ☐ Categorize the most important aspects of your life into "buckets" (e.g., health, family, work, spirituality, art, music, creative expression)
- ☐ Write some aspirations or goals (i.e., definitions of success) for each of the areas you listed.*

- ✓ Itemize specific things you want to accomplish under each (e.g., reach an ideal body weight, get a black belt in karate, have three kids, etc.),

or

- ✓ Write an overarching success statement. (For example: "the nutrition and exercise I reward my body with give me the vitality I need to live a fully, energized life. My work allows me the freedom and autonomy to express my creativity and to positively impact those I serve.")

*I don't believe it matters exactly how you decide to write out your definitions, as long as you take the time to do it, and it feels right and inspiring for your life.

How do you know when your definition of success has evolved?

- ☐ Do you have a practice of evaluating your goals and success metrics?
- ☐ If not, consider building in some routine habits like these:
  - ✓ Find an accountability partner to share your goals with, including a regularly scheduled time to review them. As you share, consider not only your progress but also whether your commitment to it is changing.
  - ✓ Schedule quarterly reviews with yourself to go over your dreams and goals. In those reviews, ask yourself: What has changed in my life recently? Does that have any bearing on my dreams, and if so, how?
  - ✓ Mark the milestones. If you've set milestones for your dreams, use the attainment of those milestones not only to celebrate, but also to consider what's next. (For example, if your dream is to open your own business, celebrate its opening. Then ask yourself what you dream of next. Perhaps it will be a growth target for the business, but it also might be something unrelated, like travelling around the world.)

Recognition

How will you know you are successful?

Lara used a daily meal ritual as an indicator of her success, and credited it for helping her balance a successful family with a thriving business. Katie found that celebrating small wins helped her gain confidence to go after her bigger dream to make a living as an artist.

How do you recognize your success?

- ☐ Consider the items you listed under your definition of success. Is there a way you can measure your progress?

- ☐ Give each item a value if the measure of success is tangible, like the number of kids you want, the amount of money you want to make, or the pounds you need to lose.

- ☐ If the measure is not tangible, focus on your progress by asking yourself, "Am I moving this goal forward? Am I happy with the outcome today? Is this where I want it to be?"

- ☐ What steps have you already taken in your effort toward your goals? Remember to recognize making a decision, saying an intention out loud, or sharing your dreams with someone as progress. Sometimes starting is the scariest part.

Are you celebrating your small wins and your "perfect shots"?

If not, consider these methods:

- ☐ Each evening when you lie down to sleep, make a habit of reviewing your day. Ask yourself, "What am I most proud of today?" or say, "I am so grateful that I was able to accomplish _____ today."

- ☐ At the end of each week, make a habit of writing down your biggest accomplishment of the week. Put it on a sticky note and place the note on your bathroom mirror or somewhere you will see it regularly. Use the small wins from the previous week to inspire you for the upcoming week.

- ☐ At the end of the month, find a way to reward yourself for the month's accomplishments. Invite friends over to celebrate your success, or give yourself extra time to do something you love but don't get enough time to squeeze in (like a massage, a stroll through a park, or a movie).

Chapter 8: Highway to Happiness

Most folks are as happy as they make up their minds to be.

Abraham Lincoln

Shortly after I left my corporate career to "find myself," I hired a life coach to help me. I knew I was on a path to finding more meaning and purpose in my life, but I really had no idea how to actually go about doing that. During one of the first conversations I had with the life coach, she asked me, "What brings you joy?" The question that brought me to tears. I had absolutely no idea. How sad is that? The "people-pleaser" side of me immediately started to think of answers I thought she wanted to hear. I know that's even sadder, but it's true. When I mentioned a few different things I liked, she stopped me and once again said, "No, that's not the same. What brings you joy?"

That single question became a symbol of my journey, and although I can't exactly remember, it probably led to the phrase "Finding Fabulous." In that moment, my goal for the immediate future changed from finding a new career to finding out what brings me joy. Part of me just wanted to find an answer in case anyone ever asked me again, but mostly I longed to live a joyous life that would eliminate the need for the question in the first place.

In my effort to understand the outcomes of going through a major transformation, I initially focused on asking the FabFinders for their definitions of success. I didn't start out asking if they were happy, but many of their answers (some more than others) organically led to a discussion about happiness. Some of them use happiness as the overarching umbrella of their success, while others spoke of it more as an element. It had me wondering if they are inextricably connected. Can you be successful and not happy? Conversely, can you be happy and not successful?

In an effort to find and understand my own joy, I followed the breadcrumbs left by the FabFinders and found some interesting commonalities on their path to greater happiness. Whether they had already found their full version of Fabulous or not, they taught me some key components to ensuring happiness was part of the journey:

- **Meaning & Impact of Happiness**
- **Finding Happiness**
- **Importance of Checkpoints**

In the previous chapter, we discussed success as a journey, not a destination. In this chapter I want to challenge you to think about the role of happiness in that process. If we get too focused on checking things off a list of wants or things we want to accomplish, we can lose the forest for the trees. The journey of Finding Fabulous can be challenging at times, but it is meant to bring more joy into our lives. I hope that you experience that happiness along the way and take the time to appreciate how your happiness benefits everyone around you.

Meaning & Impact of Happiness

> *Happiness is when what you think, what you say, and what you do are in harmony.*
>
> Gandhi

Happiness as an Umbrella of Success

Does getting everything you want make you happy, or does being happy lead to getting everything you want? It is, perhaps, akin to the proverbial "chicken and egg" conundrum. As I contemplated the dilemma, I debated whether or not I needed to write a separate chapter about happiness. After all, we just spoke about defining our own success and what it means to live that definition—doesn't that cover it? If we are really successful on our own terms, won't we be happy by default?

To be honest, I don't know the answer to that question, but after interviewing all the FabFinders, one thing I *am* certain of is that it's not necessary to have everything you want to be happy. That isn't to say you wouldn't be happier if you could have, be, and do all the things you want, but I've learned that happiness can be a choice, a state of mind, and something that can be picked up along the way. From the first moment I decided to leave my job (months before I actually left), I was happier. The choice to act instead of settle made me happier. Through days and months when I struggled to figure out what I was going to do, during all the times I fought back self-doubt and grappled with self-confidence, I was still happier than I was settling in my old corporate job.

I wasn't alone. A lawyer-turned-marketing manager knew she wasn't working in a role she would perform forever, yet she told me she was happier than ever. The chiropractor who wanted to open her own birthing centres radiated so much joy, despite being years away from actually accomplishing that goal. The fact that she had walked away from a situation that didn't match her values was enough to increase her happiness.

Tom's Story

Tom was one of the first FabFinders to speak about happiness as an overarching measure of success and his number one goal. The way he leverages his feelings of happiness to make decisions and course corrections is a lesson for all of us.

You don't have to speak to Tom for very long before you realize that he's man on a mission—a man who, at the relatively young age of twenty-eight, is wise beyond his years. Enviably, he has already figured out the key: success is not measured in dollars, but in attainment of happiness.

Tom started working for his father's commercial real estate and property management business straight out of college. It took him only five short years to realize he was on the wrong path. Sure, he was successful at the work he did, and was proving to himself and his father that he could earn his place in that company if he chose to. However, something was missing. Inspired by his father's entrepreneurism, Tom learned at a young age the benefits of working for yourself. He intuitively knew that if he wanted to have control over his time and his legacy, he needed to start his own company. Realizing that he was nowhere near attaining, or even initiating, that goal, Tom decided to make a change.

He kept his ambitions to himself for the first six months, attempting to start an online business that would eventually allow him to quit his job. Fearing what his friends and family, particularly his father, would think, he started that business quietly in his spare time. Although he views those first attempts as failures, he learned a lot in the process. He firmly believes that the path to success is paved with failures, and that applying the knowledge and experience you gain from them eventually leads to your greatest success.

Despite the fact that his business was only making a few hundred dollars a month at the time, Tom finally quit his job. As predicted, his father was surprised, disappointed, and worried, but in the end he was also proud that Tom had taken the leap of faith and gone after what he really wanted.

When the conversation turned to Tom's definition of success, it becomes clear just how grounded, self-assured, and wise he really is. As he's gone through the stages of developing his business, and his earnings have grown every month, he has learned something really valuable. Once he reached a monthly income large enough to pay his bills, everything above and beyond that amount became less important. Although he recognizes a certain amount of money is necessary for living, and he won't turn riches away if they come, his happiness is tied more closely to helping others. It has become the filter that determines his choices. Demonstrating just how committed he is to this principle, he chose to close down certain aspects of his business because they weren't making him happy, even though they were adding steady income to his bottom line.

His definition of success is, quite simply, happiness. As his products and services evolve, he continually asks the question, "Is this making me happy?" If the answer is "no," he adjusts his efforts accordingly. Focusing his time on things that excite and interest him—and ignoring other peoples' opinions of his "successes"—feeds that happiness and ultimately allows him to help more people.

Tom explained that people often compete with each other in terms of how big their homes are, their income levels, or other material things, and associate that "success" with happiness. I agree with his assessment that it is ridiculous, if not impossible, to compare your happiness with someone else's. Since you can't compete, it leaves you with only your own happiness as a guide. Does this make me happy? Am I happier than I was yesterday? Is there something I would like to have, or do, or be, which could add to my happiness? The awareness that comes from asking yourself these questions brings you closer to the answers.

> Tom summed it up by saying, "If, at the end of my life, I can say I spent my time pursuing and achieving happiness, and helping others find their happiness, what's a better life lived?"

Tom's actions quite intentionally move him toward being happier. His philosophy reflects the main message I want to convey with this book: the "finding" part of Finding Fabulous is all about action. Beyond all the other lessons we've discussed, I'm proposing that, in and of itself, taking action toward what you want to have, be, or do will lead to a more fabulous life. FabFinders validated this idea when they spoke of how happy they were simply to have started the journey, regardless of how close they were to attaining their ultimate dreams. Even though a few of them wished they had done things differently, I couldn't find one person who regretted the decision or wished to go back and take a different path. To me, the happiness that comes with that is the true sign of success.

How does our happiness impacts others?

> *Some cause happiness wherever they go;*
> *others whenever they go.*
>
> **Oscar Wilde**

I remember walking into a grocery store several years ago in a really foul mood. I don't remember why, or even what I went in to buy. I just remember feeling really cranky. Scanning the store to find my item, I turned down an aisle and stopped dead in my tracks. There, alone in the aisle, was a little girl, about five or six years old, skipping along, singing "Rudolph the Red-Nosed Reindeer" at the top of her lungs. It must have been summer, because the pure joy in her tone was accentuated by the odd timing of the tune. Not missing a beat, she looked up at me, smiled, and kept skipping along toward the other end of the store. The laughter that escaped me in that moment miraculously took my bad mood with it!

Have you ever been in the presence of a person who was so happy that you just couldn't help but be happy too? Moods and energy are contagious, including happiness. Whether happiness fits your overall idea of success or not, know that your happiness is capable of making someone else's day.

Karen is one of the FabFinders who taught me about appreciating another person's enthusiasm and happiness. If I had met her several years ago, I probably would have thought she was a bit too "woo woo" for my tastes, but since I happened to meet her at a time in my life when my curiosity trumped my scepticism, my reaction to her was completely different. Although she started out doing fairly conventional jobs like working for a printing company and marketing promotional paraphernalia, Karen ended up with a somewhat nontraditional career. Specializing in Reiki, yoga, meditation, and aromatherapy, along with her other intuitive talents, she is what some would call an alternative healer.

I met Karen a few years ago at a networking event for entrepreneurial women, when she was giving a talk about the benefits of vibrational water. With my background in pharmaceuticals—where a double-blind, placebo-controlled study of thousands of patients is often not enough to convince physicians of a medicine's efficacy—you can imagine what I thought as she explained the effectiveness of placing earphones on water bottles. She asserted that drinking water that has been exposed to different vibrational sounds can heal the body of indigestion, flu virus, and even cancer. Despite my sceptical knee-jerk response, I found myself fascinated by the woman who was giving such a heartfelt explanation. She was so excited! Happiness, enthusiasm and an unshakeable confidence emanated from her very being. It was obvious how much she believed in the unusual treatment and how happy she was to share the results with us. In that moment, I knew that, whether or not I was completely sold on the water itself, I was witnessing the impact that someone's happiness can have on others. I didn't need to drink the water; I felt better just listening to her! Still unclear about my own purpose at the time, the experience gave me a new sense of hope and inspired me to keep looking for the one thing that could make me vibrate with even a fraction of the happiness that radiated from this extraordinary woman.

Is our own happiness selfish or selfless?

If you've ever been on a commercial flight, you're probably familiar with the safety instructions the crew gives about the oxygen masks. In the off chance the plane's cabin depressurizes during the flight, oxygen masks will fall from the overhead compartment. The flight attendants instruct anyone travelling with small children or others needing assistance to put on their own masks before helping anyone else. Although some might consider this a selfish act, there is good reason for the instruction. A depressurized cabin can cause a person to pass out (hence the reason for the oxygen). If you try to apply someone else's mask before your own, you could pass out before you get the other person's mask in place. If you pass out, what help can you offer to anyone else?

I think oxygen is kind of like happiness. Thinking of someone else's happiness above your own may seem like a selfless thing to do. However, if you are not truly happy, how can you help someone else with his or her happiness? In other words, how can you give what you don't have?

Reflecting on conversations I've had with parents over the past few years, I'm reminded of this paradox. Often parents would tell me they couldn't do what they really wanted because of their children. Finances, time, and energy are prioritized for the kids. Although I respect the good intentions of these actions, I can't help wondering what message that sends to the children. You wouldn't say, "I'm going to concentrate on making my children kind and honest, and once they are, then I will also be that way." Being kind and honest yourself allows you to model the very behaviours you wish for in your children, so why would it be any different with happiness? How can you teach a child that being happy is important if you don't prioritize (at least to some extent) your own happiness? If it's true that children learn what they live, doesn't it stand to reason that growing up with happy parents would provide fertile ground for happy children?

Although my opinion on this matter may not hold much weight (since I don't have children of my own), I do think the overall concept of happiness is an important one on the road to Finding Fabulous. Think about Mikey, the HR director who was so miserable he would cry in his office. Even though he tried to hide that from his family, he was called out by his ten-year-old daughter. He had been trying to instil the importance of being engaged and happy to his family, but he hadn't been living the principles himself. How well do you think he was able to convey that message to his four kids? Additionally, considering that he was the director of an HR department, how well do you think he was able to create a happy work environment for the employees during that time?

As I share the ideas around the journey of *Finding Fabulous* with people I meet, they often recount all the reasons they can't do it themselves. Typically, when they list all the things they could lose if they make a major career shift, they make it sound like the decision would be a selfish one. They say their kids won't be able to go to hockey camp, or the family won't be able to afford their large home. They might tell me how expensive it is for the family to go on vacation, or how much the kids' new iPad just cost them. It appears that a lot of people think the decision to be happier is selfish.

What would happen if they shifted their focus? What could their families gain if they were happier people? What if their kids could have parents who were not only around more often, but also happier when they were? What difference could it make to a marriage if both spouses came home happier and excited to share their days? If more people knew their happiness would ultimately benefit their families in new and unexpected ways, would they be more willing to make the change? Would they be less likely to think their transformation was selfish? Would the so-called "bad" be more acceptable with a full appreciation of how *good* the good could be?

Finding Happiness

> *For the past thirty-three years, I have looked in the mirror every morning and asked myself: "If today were the last day of my life, would I want to do what I am about to do today?" And whenever the answer has been "no" for too many days in a row, I know I need to change something.*
>
> Steve Jobs

In the corporate world, it's a common practice during business planning to set S.M.A.R.T. goals. For those who aren't familiar with the concept, S.M.A.R.T. stands for Specific, Measurable, Attainable, Relevant, and Time-bound. It is a way to ensure that we work toward goals that matter and that can be measured. Although that practice is somewhat effective, I think it misses the mark when it's used to create the really big, and arguably the most important, goals. I wonder if this popular goal-evaluating framework can apply to happiness. Is it S.M.A.R.T. to want to achieve ultimate happiness?

When you think about it, happiness itself is not exactly a specific goal. After all, happiness for me may be completely different from what it means for you. What happiness looks like today can be completely different from what it meant last year or the year before. Assume for a moment that we could create a specific definition for the kind of happiness we wanted. Would we be able to measure it? I've never found an instrument or ruler that can compare my happiness to someone else's, or measure how much it increased or decreased over time. How about attainable? That one I will concede; otherwise what are we all living for? If I didn't think it was relevant I wouldn't have devoted an entire chapter to the concept, but I wonder if it is time-bound. Would you ever say, "I need to be this happy by this Tuesday or I've failed to reach my goal?"

Let's face it: happiness is not the most tangible goal we could create for ourselves. Happiness, like love, joy, gratitude and every other emotion, isn't something we can put a number on. However, I think Steve Jobs had it right: the best way to measure happiness is to look at yourself in the mirror. Whether or not he was happy doing what he was doing in his everyday life, he was able to use his own happiness as a benchmark for how he lived his life, and he did that every day. How many of us leverage that same simple technique?

When I contemplate how useful this could be for my own pursuit of happiness, I remember all the FabFinders who had to follow the breadcrumbs toward their passions. Understanding what made them happy along the way helped them move toward it and allowed them to get where they are today. An architect realized he was happier working with the people meant to fill his buildings than with the buildings themselves. In his mission to inspire individuals to live their purpose, he followed his own joy and fascination, moving from architecting buildings to architecting people. When Julia realized how much happier she was giving presentations to parenting groups, it gave her reason enough to step away from a long career as a youth and family counsellor. She found happiness in the simple act of being able to express her true self in a new environment. Although I didn't fully understand what could make me happy when I left the corporate world, I had my own version of Steve Job's mirror question, and I didn't like the answer for far too many days in a row.

What is your level of happiness telling you? When you are most happy, what are you doing, who are you being, and where are you spending your time? Could those moments of happiness be laying down breadcrumbs on the path toward your best life?

Time to Be Happy

> *If you wait for the perfect moment when all is safe and assured, it may never arrive. Mountains will not be climbed, races won, or lasting happiness achieved.*
>
> **Maurice Chevalier**

"Once I am married and settled down, then I'll be happy."

"As soon as my children graduate, then I can do something that makes me happy."

"As soon as I get that promotion and start making more money, then I'll be happy."

"After I retire I will have all the time in the world to do things that make me happy."

Do any of these sound familiar?

Why do we put off our happiness? What are we waiting for?

One of the physicians in the territory I used to manage found out, the same month he decided to retire, that he had StageFour cancer. All he talked about during the months before his diagnosis was how much he was looking forward to being able to spend all his time golfing. He died a year later. It's a tragic story that provides a great lesson: we don't know when our time will be up. The only sure thing is that this time will never come again. I once heard a motivational speaker sum it up this way: "This is not a dress rehearsal; this is your real life." When I think about that physician's life, I hope he was happy. I hope that being a physician for the majority of his life was what made him truly happy. I know that golf made him happy too, but I'd like to think he didn't wait for happiness until that one year of retirement.

As I think about my own life, I wonder if I waited too long to be happy. How many years did I waste waiting for something or someone to come along and make me happy? Any time I met a young FabFinder, a flash of envy would come over me and I would think, "Good for you, not waiting so long to make happiness your priority!" After all, Tom worked for his father for only five years before he took his leap of faith, and Janel spent about the same amount of time as an engineer before she followed her joy for horses. But then, as the universe often does, I'd be shown the opposite perspective by meeting people who were mere years away from retirement when they took their first brave steps. Overall, it was encouraging to see FabFinders who represented such a wide variety of ages, number of working years, and amounts of time between decision and action.

They taught me that it doesn't matter. It doesn't matter if you work five or twenty-five years before you figure it out. It doesn't matter if you transition immediately or take years to do it. What matters is deciding what timing is right for you. What matters more is that you don't use time as an excuse to hold you back. "I'm too young," "I'm too old," "I'm nowhere near retirement," or "I'm too close to retirement," are all just excuses. If you take nothing else away from the stories of the FabFinders, I hope you've learned that Finding Fabulous is possible at any time, for anyone. You just have to say, "It's my time!" and it will be!

Happiness as a Navigation Tool

> *Happiness is not something ready-made.*
> *It comes from your own actions.*
>
> **Dalai Lama XIV**

When it comes to food, I'm not very disciplined. I have this crazy sweet tooth, and it has a tendency to rule my kitchen. This year I decided that I wanted to put more priority on eating right, because I believe it can have a huge impact on my happiness. I believe that the increased vitality I could get from the right nutrition would give me the energy I need to do the rest of the things I love to do. It didn't take long for me to recognize that I needed to learn how to shop and cook differently if I was going to make a big difference. The only problem: old habits die hard! Who has time for that? Although I started off with the best of intentions, it wasn't long before my grocery store visits turned into zombie-like re-enactments in which I'd place the same old ingredients in my cart time and time again. I needed something simpler to get off to the right start. That's when I decided to cut sugar out of my diet. I thought if I could go without sugar for at least thirty days, I could gain a heightened awareness and start new habits that would last.

That decision produced benefits far beyond my expectations. Aside from helping me eat healthier, it gave me an incredible sense of control and freedom. All of a sudden it was so simple to decide what to eat. Does it have sugar? Easy decision. Pop or water? Easy decision. Cookies or fruit? Easy decision. It was so simple to follow. I didn't have to fill my daily quota of decision-making or use any extra brainpower to stick to that diet.

I'm not telling you this to imply anything about the proper diet or to suggest that you go off sugar; I'll let the nutritionists battle over that. However, that experience taught me something useful for my journey of Finding Fabulous: the choice to follow an unconventional path is full of decisions. Should you leave your job? Should you become an entrepreneur? How much money should you save before you take the leap? How supportive does your spouse need to be before you decide? There are so many questions you need to answer and choices you need to make. Honestly, it can be overwhelming, so how can you make it less so? Give yourself a "sugar or no sugar" decision-making tool, only this time, the question becomes, "Will this make me happy?" or, "Will this add to my happiness?"

Tom spoke about how this decision-making tool helped him figure out the direction for his business. Despite his growing income, he found himself doing things that didn't excite him, so he asked himself, "If I made less money, but didn't have to do this part of my job, would I be happier?" The same method worked for other decisions in his life. He would think about taking a trip to London to visit his old roommates and decide, "Yes, spending the money on that trip would make me happy," or he'd walk by his garden and think, "Yes, investing some time to clean it up would make me happier every time I walk by." Asking the simple question, "Will this add to my happiness?" became the standard for all his decisions.

I firmly believe that following our bliss is the only way to truly serve the world the way we are meant to. Getting distracted by the whims, desires, and agendas of others will do the opposite. How can you possibly fulfill your purpose if you are constantly bending to the aspirations of others? Get in the habit of asking the basic question, "Will this add to my happiness?" and it can guide you in the right direction. There is a reason you love the things you love; happiness is the way the universe speaks to us. Why does writing make me happy? Is it because I'm meant to write? Why does healing make doctors happy? Is it so they will? Why does cracking jokes bring happiness to comedians? Could it be they are meant to lighten the mood and bring laughter to the world? Happiness is a game changer. Not only does it simplify your ability to make your own decisions, it also gives you permission to say no or change course when necessary.

Although this line of thinking might initially seem selfish, remember how contagious happiness can be. You have a finite number of hours in the day and a limited amount of energy you can expend. How will you direct that time and energy toward things that bring you happiness? How could following your bliss impact your journey of Finding Fabulous?

Importance of Checkpoints

> *Now and then it's good to pause in our pursuit of happiness and just be happy.*
>
> Guillaume Apollinaire

As we just discussed, happiness is not one of those things that's easily measured, nor is it something you can easily compare to someone else. What makes you happy may not make me happy, and vice versa. The best thing about that is that it frees you from playing the comparison game. There is no "keeping up with the Joneses" in terms of happiness. Despite that, I do believe there are multiple benefits in monitoring just how happy you are.

What makes you happy today might not make you happy tomorrow. The stories from the FabFinders have illustrated this over and over again throughout this book. Some FabFinders were happy with their early careers, until they weren't. Travel and long hours added excitement and joy to the pursuits and ambitions of corporate women until they had children. Chasing a title or fame and fortune brought joy until revelations of new talents carved out new possibilities. Happiness can change over time.

When I walked away from my corporate job, I left behind much more than just a salary. The first Monday I was officially a free woman, I was standing at the gas pumps when a thought occurred to me: it was the first time in years that I was going to be paying for my own gas. Yikes! Sad, I know, but such is life with a company car! As I slipped my credit card into the automated pump, I paused for a moment of self-reflection. "What have I done? I have no job, no salary, no plans to have a job or salary anytime soon, and yet I will still have to put gas in my car. Am I okay with that?" It took maybe one full second to come up with, "Yep! I'd still rather pay for my own gas than be stuck in that job!"

That one moment of pure faith and knowing has helped me through many moments over the past couple of years. Any time I feel frustrated with my lack of clarity, anxious about my declining bank account, or doubtful about when it will all come together, I think of the sensation of inserting that credit card into that gas pump. I pause, ask myself the same questions, and a hundred percent of the time, I come up with the same answer. I'd still rather be here in this moment, no matter how challenging. I'm so much happier dealing with the problems I have today than the ones I had in "those" days. It has occurred to me more than once that the pure action of moving toward something you want can give you the sensation of already having it. Experience taught me how true the opposite is, where staying in a bad situation leaves you feeling nothing but stuck. Now I have proof of the counterpoint. Maybe that in and of itself will be my greatest success: learning that the secret to happiness is moving toward it while simultaneously realizing you've already found it.

Happiness can be a great indicator to help you stay on track. It's as if we all have this built-in system that directs our choices toward our best life if we listen to it. Tapping into how we feel when we are in certain places, get to be specific ways, do particular tasks, or spend time with different people can give us clues to Finding Fabulous. It can also provide the much-needed motivation to stay the course when things get tough. That's what my "gas pump" moment was for me.

What does that look like for you? Do you have a similar experience that helps you stay on track when things get hard?

Celebration & Gratitude

> *But what is happiness except the simple harmony between a man and the life he leads?*
>
> **Albert Camus**

When I chose to take a cross-country road trip with my dog, I threw a bunch of camping equipment in my car and set off with only a sketch of a plan. I knew I was going to cut across the US toward Yellowstone Park before heading up to the Canadian Rockies and then down again along the Oregon and California coasts. Along the way, I planned to visit a few old friends, catch up on some writing, and spend some time playing tourist at famous landmarks like Mount Rushmore and Lake Louise. Other than that, I was open to wherever the road would lead us and whoever we would meet along the way. I had no commitments and no timelines. I was truly free!

On the first day of that journey, I made a stop in a small town in Michigan. There was a gorgeous waterfront park and beautiful sandy beach that stretched for miles. It was mid-September, and most people I knew were headed back to school or settling back into post-vacation work schedules, and there I was standing on a beach smiling at the lake. As I stood on the shores of Lake Michigan—light breeze blowing through my hair, sunshine warming my face—all I could feel was pure gratitude. I didn't *think* about being grateful, I *felt* it! With every cell in my body, I felt grateful. Almost overwhelmed by the feeling, I knew, in that moment, that I was on the path to my best life.

Perhaps my pure curiosity and desire for adventure made me more open to it that day, but it may have been the first real celebration of my choice. Remember, this was ten months after I left. Why did it take me so long? Sure, I was happy with my decision from the start, but I don't think I fully appreciated what I had done and what it could mean for me until I stood on that shoreline.

Some of my favourite moments with the FabFinders happened when I'd catch them remembering their own "shoreline" moments. I think of the tutor who had tears in her eyes as she recounted the success of one of her students, and the pride in the eyes of the golf instructor as she explained how her clients' success on the course was translating into other areas of their lives. I can feel the joy radiating from the life coach who learned to dream again, and I can hear the giggle in the voice of the online marketing expert as she tells me her eighty-nine-year-old mother had started blogging and selling products online. These are the moments that make it all worthwhile. These are moments we have to celebrate. The joy, happiness, and gratitude that accompany these moments should be savoured, celebrated, and remembered. They not only help us know we are on course, they also remind us why we are doing it.

We don't have to wait for some major milestone, or even some extreme instance of happiness, in order to celebrate. Making a habit out of recognizing when we're happy can counterbalance all the times we're frustrated and anxious. Those uncomfortable feelings may be an inevitable part of going through major transformations, but they become more manageable when we increase the time and energy we spend in gratitude for the things that make us happy.

Stopping to feel your happiness, sharing your happiness with others, or creating your own ritual for marking that happiness are all methods of bringing more focus to it. What could you accomplish if you allowed yourself to be happier on a more consistent basis? How can you leverage your happy moments in your journey of Finding Fabulous?

Roadmap: Finding Happiness Along the Way

Whether you use happiness as an overarching measure of your success or you just want it to be a component, happiness is key in *Finding Fabulous*. From helping to guide our decisions and stay the course when things get tough, to reminding us to celebrate our wins, this concept of happiness warrants our time and energy.

Let's get clear on the role that happiness can play in helping you along your transformational journey.

- Meaning and Impact of Happiness
- Finding Happiness
- Importance of Checkpoints

Let's peel back the layers of your happiness:

Meaning & Impact

What does happiness mean for you?

Tom's story is a great example of how happiness can be an umbrella for success. In his case, he uses his happiness to guide his decisions and monitor his progress.

- ☐ Have you taken any time to really consider what happiness means to you?
    - ✓ Consider the equation of success you created in the last chapter. Where does happiness fit amongst other things? How high a priority is it?
    - ✓ Spend some time journaling your feelings on happiness in terms

of whether you would like it to be a yard stick for your success or simply a by-product.

- ☐ Who might benefit from your happiness?
    - ✓ Make a list of all the people in your life who are affected by your level of happiness. Think about your family, friends, co-workers, customers, etc.
    - ✓ Beside each person or group of people, write a description of how their lives could benefit from your happiness. What impact would it have on them?

Finding Happiness

How happy are you?

Every time Steve Jobs woke up and looked in a mirror, he asked himself if he was happy with what he was doing. It became a guiding principle for how he lived his life, as well as a measuring stick for just how happy he was. Gerry and Julia used their happiness to provide clues to the next step they would take on their journeys.

- ☐ Are you taking the time to check in and ask yourself how happy you are?
    - ✓ Consider using the simple Steve Jobs technique: ask yourself if you are happy doing what you are doing each day.
    - ✓ Journaling how you feel is another great way to bring more awareness to what is causing you to feel that way. Consider a nightly ritual of writing down when you were most happy during the day.
- ☐ Are you waiting for something to happen before you allow yourself to be truly happy?
- ☐ Make a list of all the things you wish for your life (finding your soul mate, opening a business, losing weight, etc.)
    - ✓ Looking over the whole list, or considering each item in turn, ask yourself what you are waiting to do as a result.

- For example: are you waiting to live in a dream home until you find your soul mate? Are you waiting to take a vacation south until you look good in a bikini?
- ✓ Decide on one action, for each item you listed, that you could take today (or this week), that would bring you more happiness as you get closer to your dreams.

☐ How could you use your happiness level to help you make decisions in your life?
- ✓ Make up one statement or question about happiness that you could use as your decision filter. (e.g. Would spending time/money/energy on this add to my happiness?)
- ✓ Try out your statement or question on some of the decisions you are trying to make right now and see how they affect your ability to move forward.

Importance of Checkpoints

So you're happy, now what?

The simple act of paying for gas reminds me to be grateful for my happiness. Perhaps it also reminds me of the cost of my decisions. Nevertheless, it is a symbol of the brave steps I took away from a situation that left me unsatisfied and unfulfilled toward one with more meaning, purpose, and fun. Anytime I am feeling overwhelmed or anxious about my future, all I have to do is close my eyes and allow myself to remember how I felt standing on that shore in Michigan. Those feelings help me celebrate my journey and remind me to be patient with my results.

☐ How can happiness help you stay the course when things get tough?
- ✓ Find a moment of pure happiness that corresponds to your decision to find fabulous.
  - If you want to spend more time with your children, think about a time when you were completely free to be with them and how it made you feel.

- If you want to positively impact others, think about a time when you were able to help someone, and how that made you feel.
- ✓ Hold that memory in your mind. Think about it in full detail: how you felt, what you saw, what you smelled, and what you could hear.
- Any time you need inspiration to keep going after your dreams, go to that place in your mind and remember what you are working toward.

☐ How will you celebrate your wins and acknowledge your happiness?
- ✓ Make a habit of celebrating your happiness by paying attention to it.
- Tell someone how happy you are.
- Post a comment about your happiness on social media.

☐ Intentionally give your happiness more attention than your setbacks or frustrations.
- Make a milestone out of your happiness by marking it with some action (for example, give yourself a high five, do a little happy dance, or play your favourite happy music).
- Slow down to really feel how happy you are (take a few full breaths as you "breathe in" the feeling, take time to meditate on the feeling, or write about it in your journal).

Conclusion

All our dreams can come true, if we have the courage to pursue them.

Walt Disney

Reflecting on the time I spent with the FabFinders, I feel blessed to have met them when I did. Even though they were all at different stages in their own journeys at the time I interviewed them, each and every one of them taught me something valuable. Hearing how their traditional, corporate, or professional jobs morphed into unique, innovative careers, I was awakened to new possibilities linked to fascinating lifestyles. Listening to how they overcame barriers and faced challenges, I came to realize that struggling toward something you want is nobler than suffering over something you don't. Most of all, I learned that success and happiness aren't elusive rewards reserved for a chosen few, but are well within our reach if we are brave enough pursue them.

Here's a summary of the lessons the FabFinders taught me:

Motivation for change drives action.

Gaining a clear understanding of why you want to change is a critical first step to getting what you want. Connecting your reasons with the results you hope to achieve can give you the momentum you need to get started, the encouragement you need to keep going, and the clarity required to focus your efforts.

Challenges are gifts.

If you let them, the challenges you encounter along the way will open up the biggest opportunities. Don't let them keep you from moving toward your best life; let them guide you along the path and direct your next steps.

Don't know what you want to do? Work on figuring it out.

Don't understand your value? Do something you value.

Don't feel credible enough? Start building your credibility, little by little.

Don't have faith you can do it? Go find someone or something you can believe in.

In debt and don't believe you can "afford" to go after your dreams? Get out of debt.

Worried about losing the lifestyle you have or giving up a lucrative salary? Change your mindset from loss to investment, and then go invest in your dreams!

Worried people will think you are crazy and won't support you? Proactively build a new support team and ask for help. Remember: support comes in many forms.

Think your skill set and experience limit your options? Widen your perception by finding examples of others doing extraordinarily different things with surprisingly ordinary talents (there are lots of them!).

Outcomes are worth it.

Success, happiness, fame or fortune; you decide. You get to redefine what it means to be successful and what your equation for happiness includes. This is your life and your story; you get to write the conclusion. Stop worrying about what others will think or believe, and start working toward what you want, what makes you feel successful, and what adds to your happiness. Decide what will make it worth it, and then go for it!

Finding Fabulous implies two things: in order to *find*, one needs to actively go looking, <u>and</u> in order to recognize it when you do, one needs to determine what *fabulous* really means.

Although the path to Finding Fabulous is winding and by no means smooth, I hope the examples and stories in this book have encouraged you to start looking. I hope you've learned that you aren't alone in this journey; the path has already been worn down by those who've gone before you. But most of all, I hope you've recognized that *Finding Fabulous* is more about the journey than the destination. And, like me, I hope you've learned that choosing to go down the path toward *Fabulous* means you've already found it!

> *The best time to plant a tree was twenty years ago.*
> *The next best time is now.*
>
> **Chinese Proverb**

Acknowledgements

This book would not have been possible without the many brave souls who were willing to share their stories with me. To those I call FabFinders, thank you for your time, patience, candor, and most of all, your trust. I will forever be grateful. Not only did you inspire me with your courage and persistence, but your examples also pave the path for others looking for a way to design their own fabulous lives. You are all a testament to the idea that Finding Fabulous is a state of mind more than any particular destination. Thanks Ann D., Alex B., Amy Ballantyne, Angela Kontgen, Beena Kavalam, Bruce Hancock, Carol Bremner, Carrie B., Carolina Caro, Chris Clark, Christine Patton, Christine D., Cindy, Connie Deckert, Darlene Huff, Darren Kenney, Della Wicklund, Geoff Affleck, Gerry Visca, Grainne Aitkin, Hala Nassif, Heather Thorkelson, Isabelle LaRue, Jacqueline Bunt, Janel Ditner, Jeremy Tracy, Jess Reid, Jessica W., Jillian R., John Lee Dumas, Jonathon, Jonathon Fields, Julia Kozusko, Karin, Katie, Katrina McGhee, Karen Egoff, Kattleya S., Kelly D., Kristoffer Carter, Lara Galloway, Leila, Lisa Reaume, Lisa Vickery, Lori W., Lori Smith, Louisa Jewell, Maren, Maria S., Martin, Megan, Melanie Schiell, Melissa, Michael C. Anthony, Mikey Nagle, Reef, Perry Gladstone, Pierrette Strudwick, Renate Donovan, Sandra O'Hagan, Sandye Brown, Scott Dinsmore, Shannon & Andy Maguire, Shelagh Cummins, Shelley Schanzenbacher, Susan Anderheggen, S. Chawla, Sue B. Zimmerman, Tania DeSa, Tanya McIntyre, Tom Ewer, Twila Kaye, Yvonne Whitelaw, and the many others I spoke to along the way.

To Carolina, who was my very first FabFinder (long before I came up with the name), I want to thank you for opening my eyes to a new way of being and always being there to remind me why I chose this path in the first place. To the rest of my California "familia," Isabelle and Kyristina, thank you for providing a loving, supportive space in which I felt free to rediscover my creative side and finally finish the book! To my new LP family, thank you for pushing me outside of my comfort zone and helping me find own my voice. You walked into my life at the perfect time, left your thumbprints on my heart, and for that I will never be the same. A special shout-out to Timothy Morse: thank you for helping me pull together the last few pieces of the puzzle that became this book. Your loving, generous nature is rare and special.

To one of my biggest mentors, and dare I say a 'FabFinder' in his own right, a huge thank-you goes out to Brendon Burchard. Although he may not have known it, he was the inspiration that led me to interview the FabFinders in the first place. Thank-you for your wisdom, your energy, your vision and most of all your big, sloppy heart! That passion you have for sharing your message with the world is not only inspiring, it's contagious!

To Marci Shimoff, Janet Bray-Attwood, and Chris Attwood, thank you for your expertise, your mentorship, and mostly, your hearts. Your dedication to supporting new authors in finding and sharing their message in an enlightened, loving way is both admirable and inspiring. To Geoff Affleck, thank you for your kindness, your advice, and most of all, your laughter. It was your simple yet profound advice to "finish your book" that taunted my thoughts and pushed me to finally get it done! To Sandye and Bruce, my enlightened mastermind partners in crime, thank you for walking with me down this journey toward authorship and keeping me laughing the whole way!

To my amazing editor, Beth Riley, thank you for keeping me on track, helping me find my voice, and for all your encouraging words throughout the process. I couldn't have done it without you!

To all my Pfizer friends (especially the Kim Crawford Club), thank you for the laughter, the tears, and the toasts! Every one of my favorite memories from those days involves you. Cathy Thomas and Martha Bellamy, I especially want to thank you for always being there to support my crazy decisions and keep me laughing through it all! Your ongoing support and encouragement mean the world to me. Sandra Wong, thank you for always opening your home to Leo and me as we ventured across the country, and for all your encouraging words as I stretched my writing muscles on that first blog. Thanks to Joel Austen for demonstrating what a fabulous boss looks like. You were an inspirational leader in an uninspiring time; thank you for the support. Melanie, my Wonder Twin, thank you for keeping me sane those last few years before I took the leap. Your friendship and support meant more than you know. Lauren, for being beside me as I put words to intention and took the leap of faith, thank you for your support and friendship.

Most of all, I want to thank my family for all the love, support, and encouragement over the past several years. Mom, you instilled confidence and perseverance in me from a young age, and for that I will forever be grateful. Thank you for finally figuring out that the best way to answer the question, "What is Lisa doing?" is to say, "Whatever she wants!" To my sister Lorraine: even though you aren't always comfortable with the ambiguity that is my life, thank you for believing in me all the same. You are my best friend, my confidant, and my definition of home; I can't do any of this without you. Wayne, thank you for having confidence in me and always cheering my success.

Nan and Pop, you have always been the pillars of our family and have taught me the value of integrity, love, and faith. Pop, you paved the path for me long before I was born, being brave enough to leave farming behind to find your own version of fabulous. I love you both more than words can express. To my aunt Carolyn and Uncle Phil, thank you for always opening your home and hearts to me, especially during Sunday dinners. You gave me a sense of grounding and stability when I needed it, and it has made all the difference. To my cousins Brad and Rob, you are the brothers I never had; thank you for always being there when I need you. To the "nieces" and "nephews" of my heart, Caitlin, Madi, Ro, and Em, your smiles and open arms fill me up and bring me pure joy. To my cousin Amy, my perpetual cheerleader, thank you for encouraging me to stay the course, kicking me in the pants when I needed it, and being the first person to actually read (and proofread) my book. Your reaction gave me the final piece of courage I needed to finally publish it!

Jenny, the word friend just doesn't cut it. You are my family, my second sister. Thank you for that uncanny sense you have of always knowing when I need you. Your love and support give me strength and reassurance. Genevieve, I guess Chianti and Leo sensed we would make great friends and brought you into my life at the perfect time. You are a great friend, and I feel like we've known each other forever. Jennifer and John, my Montreal family, you adopted me into your circle and helped me find a home away from home when I needed it most; thank you for your continued love and support.

And to all my friends who have given me love and support throughout this journey, thank you for constantly reminding me where fabulous is truly found—in the heart. I love you all!

About the Author

When she walked away from a successful career at a Fortune 100 company to find more meaning, purpose, and fun, Lisa Dadd transformed more than her job. Her decision to invest in what she was meant to *be* in life, rather than settle for what she was *doing* for a living, inspired her to interview individuals who had also turned in their day jobs to follow their passions. In her first book, *Finding Fabulous, Paving the Path between Paycheck and Passion*, Lisa shares what she learned from those interviews and dares us to consider whether or not we are living our own version of fabulous.

Taking her own advice, Lisa has intentionally redesigned her life to allow more time and flexibility to travel, learn new skills, and explore new business opportunities. Blurring the lines between work and play, Lisa's greatest inspirations have come from her adventures driving across North America with her dog and hiking to places like the Base Camp of Mt. Everest and the Inca Trail to Machu Picchu in Peru. Splitting her time between her lakefront cottage in Northern Ontario and sunny Southern California, Lisa exemplifies what *Finding Fabulous* is all about.

Currently, Lisa writes, consults and speaks on topics related to life and career redesign. Combining fifteen years of strategic business skills with real-life experience, Lisa provides practical, relevant advice for anyone tired of feeling stuck and ready to take action. To read more about her journey of Finding Fabulous, or to inquire about having her speak to your organization, visit www.lisadadd.com or email info@lisadadd.com.

Finding FabFinders

Amy Ballantyne
Speaker, Health Advocate, Mentor
www.amyballantyne.com

Angela Kontgen
Coach & Freedom Creator, Editor
www.angelakontgen.com

Beena Kavalam
Personal & Business Coach
www.coachbeena.com

Carol Bremner
Online Media Trainer & Social Media Expert
www.carolbremner.com

Carolina Caro
Executive & Corporate Coach, Author, Speaker
www.parinamaconsulting.com

Chris Clark
Founder & CEO
www.terraficionados.com

Christine Patton
Speaker, Author, Trainer in Mental Edge in Sports Performance
www.mesperf.com

Connie Deckert
LPGA Teaching Professional, Speaker
www.conniedeckert.com

Darren Kenney
Entrepreneur, Health & Wellness Expert, Speaker
www.lifesourcewellness.ca

Geoff Affleck
Marketing Strategist for Transformational Leaders & Authors
www.geoffaffleck.com

Gerry Visca
Canada's Creative Coach, Author, Inspirational Speaker, Publisher
www.gerryvisca.com

Isabelle LaRue
Creator, Host and Producer at Engineer Your Space
www.engineeryourspace.com

Grainne Aitkin
Professional Photographer
www.artandsoulcanada.com

Jacqueline Bunt
Jacqueline_Bunt@yahoo.com

Janel Ditner
Equine Bowen Practitioner, Craniosacral Therapy
www.wildaboutwellness.ca

Jeremy Tracey
Keynote Speaker & Certified World Class Speaking Coach
www.jeremytracey.com

Jessica Reid
Independent Consultant, Executive Area Manager
www.jessicareid.arbonne.com

Kelly Boyer Sagert
Content Manager & Writer / Editor at The Search Guru
www.kbsagert.com

Karen Egoff
Reiki Master, Yoga Instructor, Cranial Sacral Therapist
www.mysoulbalance.com

Kristoffer Carter
Experience & Curriculum Designer and Meditation Expert
www.thisepiclife.com

Lara Galloway
Author, Speaker, Coach
www.laragalloway.com

Lisa Reaume
Business Leadership Coach
www.lisareaume.com

Melanie Shiell
Personal Growth & Leadership Mentor
www.wibusiness.net

Michael C. Anthony
Entertaining Hypnotist, Speaker, Author, Trainer
www.michaelcanthony.com

Mikey Nagle
Career Reinvention Expert
www.mikeynagle.com

Pierrette Strudwick
Master Coach, Mentor & Speaker
www.ariseandshinecoaching.com

Renate Donovan
Executive Coach, Facilitator, NLP Coach, Hypnotist
www.emergencehypnotherapy.com

Sandra O'Hagan
Entrepreneur & Personal Training Specialist
www.sofulloflife.com

Sandye Brown
Master Certified Coach
www.wideawakeinc.com

Shannon & Andy Maguire
Digital Content Developer & Marketer
www.mattagainsttheworld.com

Shelagh Cummins
Speaker, Trainer, Business Consultant
www.shelaghcummins.com

Shelly Schanzenbacher
VP of Coaching at Synergy Management Consultants
http://inthepause.com

Susan Anderheggen
Leadership Speaker/Trainer
www.xfactorleader.com

Tanya MacIntrye
Producer / Host of The Good News Only
www.TheGoodNewsOnly.com

Tania DeSa
Passion Igniter, Leadership Coach & Trainer, TEDx Speaker
www.taniadesa.com

Tom Ewer
Freelance Writer, Entrepreneur
www.leavingworkbehind.com

Manufactured by Amazon.ca
Bolton, ON